Guitar Scales for Beginners

Learn to Solo Effortlessly!

By: Gary Nelson

Copyright © 2021

ALL RIGHTS RESERVED

No part of this book may be reproduced, stored in a retrieval system, or transmitted in any form or by any means, electronic, mechanical, photocopying, recording, scanning, or otherwise, without the prior written permission of the publisher.

Limit of Liability/Disclaimer of Warranty: the publisher and the author make no representations or warranties with respect to the accuracy or completeness of the contents of this work and specifically disclaim all warranties, including without limitation warranties of fitness for a particular purpose. No warranty may be created or extended by sales or promotional materials. The advice and strategies contained herein may not be suitable for every situation. This work is sold with the understanding that the publisher is not engaged in rendering medical, legal, or other professional advice or services. If professional assistance is required, the services of a competent professional person should be sought. Henceforth, neither the publisher nor the author shall be liable for any damages that may arise. The fact that an individual, organization or website is referred to in this work as a citation and/or potential source of further information does not mean that the author or the publisher endorses the information the individuals, organization or website may provide or recommendations they/it may make. Further, readers should be aware that websites listed on this work may have changed or disappeared between when this work was written and when it is read.

Table of Contents

Chapter 1 - Introduction 1
- What Are Guitar Scales? 2
- Are Guitar Scales Important? 3
- Practicing Scales 3
- Enhancing Creativity 4
- Better Improvisation 4
- A Word On Metronomes 5
- Moving Forward… 6

Chapter 2 - Understanding Musical Notes On The Fretboard 7
- Identifying The Fretboard's Numbered Frets 8
- Learning The Names Of The Notes On The Fretboard - The Chromatic Scale 9
- What Is The Chromatic Scale? 10

Chapter 3 - Intervals 12
- The Parts Of An Interval 13
- Perfect Interval 14
- Major Interval 14
- Minor Interval 14
- Augmented Interval 14
- Diminished Interval 15
- Internalizing Intervals With Popular Songs 17
- Minor Second - Jaws 17
- Major Second - Happy Birthday 17
- Minor Third - Greensleeves 18
- Major Third - When The Saints Go Marching In 18
- Perfect Fourth - Amazing Grace 18

Augmented 4th, Diminished 5th, Tritone - The Simpsons	19
Perfect Fifth - Twinkle, Twinkle, Little Star	19
Minor Sixth - The Entertainer	20
Major Sixth - My Bonnie Lies Over The Ocean	20
Minor Seventh - Somewhere (*West Side Story*)	21
Major Seventh - Take On Me	21
Chapter 4 - Understanding Keys	**23**
Understanding the Root	24
Notes Outside Of The Key	25
How Many Keys Are In Music?	26
An Exercise In Understanding The Tonic	26
Chapter 5 - The Major Scale	**28**
The Sound Of The Major Scale	28
The Major Scale Formula	29
Moveable Major Scale Patterns	30
Moving This Scale To A Different Key	31
The Five Major Scale CAGED Positions	32
G Major Scale - E Shape / Position 1	33
G Major Scale - D Shape / Position 2	33
G Major Scale - C Shape / Position 3	33
G Major Scale - A Shape / Position 4	33
G Major Scale - G Shape / Position 5	34
Practicing Scale Shapes	34
Three Notes Per String Major Scale Patterns	34
Chapter 6 - The Minor Scale	**39**
The Minor Scale Formula	39
Understanding Relative Minor Scales	40

A Minor Scale - Position 1 41

A Minor Scale - Position 2 41

A Minor Scale - Position 3 42

A Minor Scale - Position 4 42

A Minor Scale - Position 5 42

The Harmonic Minor Scale 42

The Harmonic Minor Scale Formula 43

When Do We Use The Harmonic Minor Scale? 44

The Melodic Minor Scale 44

Chapter 7 - The Pentatonic Scale 46

Major and Minor Pentatonic Scale Formulas 47

Pentatonic Patterns 48

Playing Over Major Chords 49

Playing Over Minor Chords 50

Playing Over Dominant Chords 50

The Blues Scale 51

Playing 12 Bar Blues 53

Chapter 8 - Major Modes 55

Major Scale Modes 56

Lydian Mode 57

The Lydian Mode In Popular Music 59

Ionian Mode 59

The Ionian Mode In Popular Music 61

Mixolydian Mode 61

Dorian Mode 64

The Dorian Mode In Popular Music 66

Aeolian Mode 67

- The Aeolian Mode In Popular Music 69
- Phrygian Mode 70
- The Phrygian Mode In Popular Music 72
- Locrian Mode 73
- The Locrian Mode In Popular Music 75
- A Summary Of the Major Scale Modes 76

Chapter 9 - Melodic Minor Modes 78
- Jazz Minor - Melodic Minor Mode 1 79
- The Jazz Minor Mode In Popular Music 80
- Dorian b2 - Melodic Minor Mode 2 81
- The Dorian b2 Mode In Popular Music 83
- Lydian Augmented - Melodic Minor Mode 3 84
- The Lydian Augmented Mode In Popular Music 86
- Lydian Dominant - Melodic Minor Mode 4 87
- The Lydian Dominant Mode In Popular Music 89
- Mixolydian b6 - Melodic Minor Mode 5 90
- The Mixolydian b6 Mode In Popular Music 91
- Locrian Natural 2 - Melodic Minor Mode 6 91
- Locrian Natural 2 In Popular Music 93
- Super Locrian - Melodic Minor Mode 7 94
- Super Locrian In Popular Music 96

Chapter 10 - Exotic Scales 97
- Arabian Guitar Scale 97
- Persian Guitar Scale 97
- Byzantine Guitar Scale 98
- Egyptian Guitar Scale 99
- Oriental Guitar Scale 99

- Japanese Guitar Scale 100
- Indian Guitar Scale 100
- Hungarian Gypsy Minor Guitar Scale 102
- Romanian Guitar Scale 102
- Hijaz Guitar Scale 103

Chapter 11 - Additional Scales 104
- Whole-Tone Scale 104
- Building The Whole-Tone Scale 104
- Practicing The Whole Tone Scale 105
- The Whole Tone Scale In Popular Music 107
- Diminished Scale 108
- Building The Diminished Scale 108
- Practicing The Diminished Scale 109

Chapter 12 - Practicing Your Scales 112
- Ascending and Descending Exercises 113
- Changing Directions 114
- Practice On One String 114
- Note Sequences 115
- Intervals 116
- Drone Practice 117
- Utilize Nursery Rhymes 118
- Sing While You Play 118
- Transcription 119
- Improvisation 119

Conclusion 120

Chapter 1 - Introduction

If you are just entering into the world of guitar, it is likely that you've heard a thing or two about scales. Unfortunately, many guitarists don't know where to start.

For starters, we wanted to say congrats for even reading this book! New guitarists typically shudder when they hear the word "scale". They think that the concept of scales is difficult or tedious. What they don't know is that scales can be tons of fun *if* you know how to use them to make music.

Maybe you have tried a few guitar scales in the past, but have wondered **why** you are trudging through the tedious task of learning them. Scales are important for a number of reasons:

- They help guitarists build strength, technique, and left and right-hand coordination.
- They act as the foundation for vocabulary, allowing guitarists to solo and improvise with ease.
- They allow guitarists to read music at a rudimentary level or higher.
- Most riffs and chords are based on scales.

For this book, we're assuming that you can play *some* guitar.

In fact, you might be pretty good at playing the guitar compared to a lot of people, but perhaps you're curious about the concepts that sit behind the notes, patterns, or riffs that you use. The scales that you are moving through might be a total mystery. Deep down inside, you know that playing would be a million times easier if you understood the general music theory behind guitar scales.

Of course, you don't need a **deep** understanding of music theory by any means.

I learned guitar when I was very young, and for a very long time I did not have any grasp of music theory. I had a great ear for music, though it wasn't until I started to dig a little deeper beyond the realm of memorizing riffs and patterns that I began to understand why certain scales functioned in certain ways.

If you don't understand the basics of music theory, you are doing yourself a true disservice.

In this book, we hope to help you grasp the concept behind guitar scale theory so that you can amp up (no pun intended) your guitar playing!

Let's dive in, shall we?

What Are Guitar Scales?

Before we get too deep in the weeds, let's define what a guitar scale is.

The dictionary defines a scale as a

"Sequence of musical notes ordered by frequency or pitch"

A guitar scale is essentially a series of musical notes that are ordered by frequency or pitch as well!

In their most basic form, scales are simply sequences of notes in ascending or descending order, which hopefully makes them seem a bit less scary.

However, it is important to note that scales are ordered using **pitches**.

Pitch is an interesting concept. It is defined as the

"Perceptual attribute which allows us to order sounds on a scale related to frequencies in either ascending or descending order"

If we put that together with our definition of the guitar scale, a scale is basically an *ordered* sequence of notes that are pitch-based.

Are Guitar Scales Important?

We hit a few bullet points discussing the importance of learning scales in the beginning, though we wanted to go a little deeper to magnify the importance.

Scales are the **building blocks of music.** Not only do they allow us to play leads and solos, but they also allow us to see which chords fit together.

Practicing Scales

There is an abundance of technical problems that can be overcome by practicing simple scales. Practicing scales can strengthen your hands while building coordination between them. You'll be able to move between chords and scales far more easily with an understanding of scales.

Including scale practice in your guitar practice routine will help you to visually organize the notes of your guitar on the physical plane so that you will have a better understanding of your fretboard too. Overall, it will enhance your ability to improvise without having to concentrate so hard. With a deeper understanding of scales, you will instead be able to focus on *other* parts of your playing, including your:

- Tone
- Dynamics
- Rhythm
- Phrasing
- … and much more!

You won't have to spend so much time worrying about whether or not the next note you play will sound good, as you'll have it drilled into your brain!

Enhancing Creativity

When you are learning licks and riffs from some of your favorite guitar players, scales will allow you to visualize what it is that you are playing. You will eventually notice that many of your favorite licks take place within specific scale patterns.

Knowing the scales will also help you to add your own creative ideas to these licks and riffs, while also creating your own. So many guitarists rely on adding the licks that they've learned into their soloing.

Why not open up the door with your improvisation instead of playing in parrot-fashion?

When you have a deeper understanding of scales, you can eventually disassociate your favorite licks from songs and move them around the fretboard to use them whenever you want! You can play them in different keys and on different strings too, which will enhance your ability to improvise.

Better Improvisation

Learning different scales will allow you to eventually mix some of your favorite scales together when improvising. When you mix scales together, you allow yourself to create more colorful, interesting solos. Of course, this doesn't happen overnight; mixing scales together during improvisation is an advanced concept that requires a lot of practice, as you must be able to visualize multiple scales at the same time.

When you get into more advanced styles of music, such as jazz, metal, or blues, you will want to have different scales available to use when you come to more colorful chords used in the progression. In the case of jazz guitar, a deep understanding of chord progressions, scales and modes is essential.

A Word on Metronomes

Before we get any deeper, I want to briefly talk about the importance of practicing all of the scales that you learn in this book with a metronome. Whether you are a beginner player or an intermediate player, metronomes are one of the most helpful musical tools around.

Beyond providing our playing with more accuracy, there are several benefits to practicing with a metronome. A very prominent advantage is that they allow us to learn with another entity in mind. If you ever plan on playing with other musicians, steady rhythm is a crucial component for you to possess. Slowing down and speeding up your scales will give you the ability to use them in a variety of situations; whether you are playing a soft, slow jazz tune, or a fast, raucous rock tune.

Metronomes also help us to focus on nuances. When you begin playing scales, it is important to start slow. This way, you can focus on getting the correct finger placement and intonation. Don't focus on speeding up until the rhythm of your scales are completely in sync with the metronome; listen to when the notes you pick line up with the metronome clicks.

Metronomes come in many forms. You can buy a physical one from your local music store or online retailer, or you can download a metronome app on any smart device. Before you move onto the lessons, get some form of a metronome to practice with.

Moving Forward...

We're glad that you've chosen this book to help you understand and master scales! Creating an understanding of the relationships between notes and chords will help you to become a better composer, songwriter, and musician.

Scales are an invaluable part of music theory and no guitar player would be complete without them.

Chapter 2 - Understanding Musical Notes on The Fretboard

For us to communicate the lessons in this book clearly, it is crucial that you have an understanding of the way that the guitar is laid out.

First, we want to cover the **open strings** to make sure you have an understanding of how the guitar is laid out **vertically.**

Having the knowledge of open note names will allow you to identify notes and intervals as we move up the neck of the guitar. Don't stress about getting all of this under your belt immediately, though it shouldn't be too difficult to grasp overall.

In **western music notation**, there are seven notes that we are going to concern ourselves with for the moment. Those notes are:

A-B-C-D-E-F-G

There are notes *in-between* those notes as well, though we'll get more into detail with that once we begin talking about the chromatic scale. For now, just keep in mind that the letters from **A-G** are representative of the seven natural musical notes.

The guitar, as you probably know, has **six** strings. Each one of those strings corresponds to a musical note. From the thickest (lowest) string to the thinnest (highest) string, the string notes read:

E-A-D-G-B-E

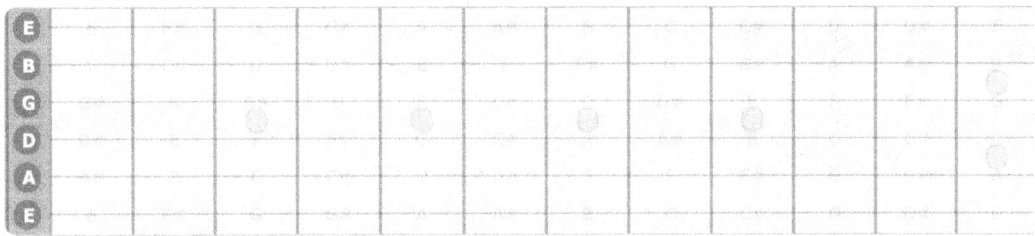

If you look at the diagram above, you will notice that the two strings on the outside are both **E** strings.

Guitar strings are often referred to by their number as well. For example, someone may refer to the high **E** string as the first string or the **D** string as the fourth string.

Identifying The Fretboard's Numbered Frets

Now that we have a good grasp on how to identify the open notes of the guitar's strings, let's begin assigning numeric identifiers to each of the guitar frets.

Take hold of your guitar. You will notice that there are a few dots or inlays on the fretboard. These dots are "position markers" and can be found on the third, fifth, seventh, ninth, and twelfth frets. Typically, you will find a double marker on the twelfth fret as well. These inlays are meant to help guitarists locate their position on the neck quickly and efficiently.

Next, take a look at the twelfth fret with the two inlays. These inlays are meant to represent the octave point on the neck. Think of the octave as having gone full circle. For example, if you are on the sixth or low E string, you know that the open string is the note **E**. When you get to the twelfth fret on that same string, you get to the **octave E**. After that, the series of notes starts all over again for the next twelve frets.

Learning the Names of the Notes on the Fretboard - The Chromatic Scale

Learning note names on the fretboard is not by any means the most thrilling topic. Though in my opinion, it is an *extremely* important one!

As a result of learning songs strictly through tablature, or learning only by ear, guitarists will often have a huge blind spot in their guitar playing: fretboard geography. That is, knowing the notes of the fretboard. It would be **insane** to find a piano player who didn't know the names of the notes on the keys that they are playing. Unfortunately, many guitarists are fine with the fretboard being some mysterious black hole of notes.

I believe there are a few reasons why this is true. For starters, becoming familiar with the notes is hard work, especially due to the fact that the guitar is tuned oddly. Second/furthermore, the guitar, in many ways, is an instrument that is based on patterns. Many guitarists think in terms of chord shapes or inlays rather than the names of the notes that they are playing. The obscurity of tablature isn't the biggest help either.

Of course, there is nothing actually wrong with learning patterns or using tablature to help you when learning a song. In fact, patterns help us build flexibility around the neck and give us our "get out of jail free cards" when we need to buy time during improvisation. However, knowing the fretboard and its notes is critical if you want to have an in depth understanding of scales.

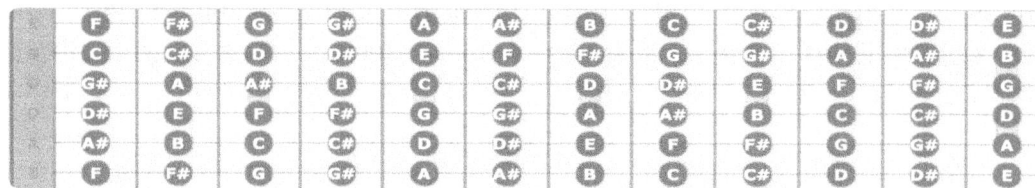

Ahh, that looks like a lot of fun, doesn't it?

We have gone over the open notes of the guitar strings to gain a better understanding of the guitar **vertically**, now let's begin moving up the neck to gain a better understanding of the guitar **horizontally**.

To do this, we must talk about the **Chromatic Scale.**

What Is The Chromatic Scale?

As you will soon find out, there are many different types of scales in the world of music. Some have five notes, some have seven, some sound triumphant, and some sound like a death march. However, there is one scale that is the foundation for all others, which uses all twelve pitches found in western music (including those in between the eight natural notes that we discussed before).

That scale is known as the **chromatic scale**.

The chromatic scale is a pretty simple concept: it is all twelve possible notes arranged in either ascending or descending pitch order. The scale is made *entirely* out of **semi-tones,** also known as **half-steps,** with each note being the smallest increment up or down after the one before.

The chromatic scale, starting from the note **C**, looks like this:

C C# D D# E F F# G G# A A# B C

Let's look at the layout of the chromatic scale on the sixth (**E**) string:

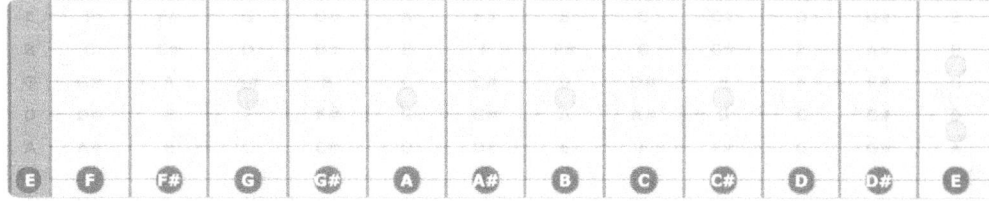

As you can see, in this instance, the chromatic scale on the **E** string moves in the same pattern as the **C** chromatic scale, though it starts on **E** rather than **C**.

While most musical scales must be notated in particular ways, you can notate a chromatic scale in a number of ways using **accidentals**.

An accidental in music is a symbol that modifies the pitch of a note. There are three different accidentals commonly used in music:

-Flat (b), which is used to *lower* a note a half step.
-Sharp (#), which is used to *raise* a note a half step.
-Natural (♮), which is a note that has not been altered.

So, take a look at the fretboard diagram above with all chromatic notes on the low **E** string. If we were to look at the note **C#**, for example, we would know that it is one half-step above the *natural* note **C**.

Now, keeping that in mind, let's find the correct spot for the note **Db**. **Db** is one half-step below **D**. If you look at the fret diagram above, you might be thinking,

"Wait a minute, then both C# and Db land in the same place...what gives?!"

This is because they are **enharmonic equivalents**, meaning they both share the same pitch and can be found in the same place on the fretboard. Choosing to use one instead of the other depends on the *context,* which we will get into later when we discuss different scales. But for now, the general rule of thumb in music is: use *sharps* when *ascending* in pitch; use *flats* when *descending* in pitch.

The chromatic scale with all **enharmonic equivalents** looks something like this:

C	C#/Db	D	D#/Eb	E	F	F#/Gb	G	G#/Ab	A	A#/Bb	B	C

Chapter 3 - Intervals

Intervals are the **foundation** of scales.

Intervals are a foundational concept in the musical world; they are building blocks that allow us to construct scales and create melodies. With that said, the theory that is wrapped around intervals can get very involved, very quickly.

Before we dive in and define our different melodic intervals, let's make sure that you have an understanding of what an interval is.

In music theory, an interval is the space that lies between two pitches.

Bring that definition to the guitar fretboard and you could switch it up to read:

On the guitar, an interval is the space between two notes on the fretboard.

For example, look at the interval below:

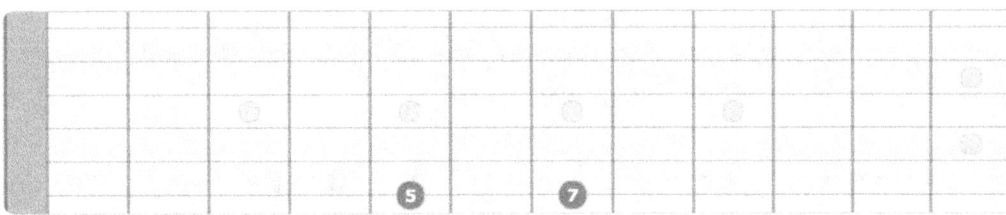

The notes that you see are separated by **two semitones**. On the guitar, a semitone is equal to the movement of one fret. A **semitone** can also be referred to as a **half-step**. Therefore, **two semitones** are equal to a **whole-step**.

Of course, intervals don't *have* to be on the same string. For example, look at the next interval below:

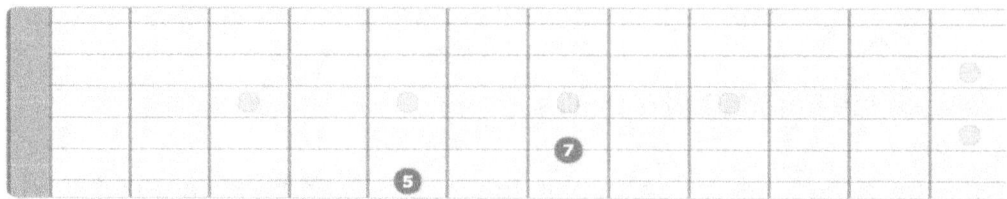

To figure out what this interval is, we first have to learn what makes up an interval.

The Parts of an Interval

Like we said before, intervals are very simple.

In fact, they only consist of two parts:

- A **number**
- A **prefix**

The number represents the distance from the first pitch to the second pitch. For example, let's say we want to figure out the interval from **G** to **A**. We make sure that we include the first note in our counting, so in this case we would count "G, A", which gives us two notes. Therefore, our interval is a **second**.

Here's another example. If we are moving from **F** to **A**, that distance covers three pitches, **F-G-A**. This makes this interval a **third**.

As we continue moving through the series of notes (**C-D-E-F-G-A-B**), we continue this same naming pattern, with the exception of an interval from one pitch to the *same* pitch, which is known as a **unison**. Look at the diagram below to see the intervals of the C Major Scale, which has no sharps or flats, all notes are natural.

Perfect Unison | Major 2nd | Major 3rd | Perfect Fourth | Perfect Fifth | Major 6th | Major 7th | Perfect Octave

Above is where we see the interval's **prefix,** which is based on the **quality** of the interval (more on that later). Since the example above is a Major scale, the only prefixes used are **Perfect** and **Major**.

Here are all the possible prefixes for intervals and their definitions. It is important to note that when you change an interval's prefix, the sound will change but the number doesn't change.

Perfect Interval

A **perfect interval** includes unisons, octaves, perfect fifths, and perfect fourths. Perfect intervals are labeled with the letter "**P**".

Major Interval

A **Major** prefix is used when you have a second, third, sixth, or seventh. These intervals reflect the second, third, sixth, and seventh notes in a major scale. Major intervals use the prefix "**M**" (note that it is UPPERCASE), or sometimes "**Maj**", or "**Δ**".

Minor Interval

A **Minor** interval occurs when you take a major interval and make it one half-step lower. Minor intervals are labeled with the prefix "**m**" (note that it is *lowercase*), "**min**", or "**-**".

Augmented Interval

An **augmented** interval occurs when you take a *major* or *perfect* interval and you make it one half-step higher. An augmented interval's prefix can be labeled with an "**A**", "**Aug**", or with a "**+**" sign. If we took the P5 from the C Major scale, which is **C** to **G**, and changed it to **C** to **G#**, we would be changing it to an augmented fifth, which we would notate as **A5**.

Diminished Interval

A **Diminished** interval occurs when you take a perfect or minor interval and make it one half-step smaller. A diminished interval can be labeled with the prefix "**dim**", "**d**", or with a "**°**" symbol (similar to a measurement of degrees). If we took the **P5** from the C Major scale again, (**C** to **G**) and changed it to **C** to **Gb**, we would be making it a diminished fifth, which we would notate as **d5**. A diminished fifth is also referred to as the **tritone**, which has significance in music history as being one of the most dissonant intervals.

Remember, an interval has two different notes: a top pitch and a bottom pitch. You can change an interval by altering the top note *or* the bottom note.

Look at the diagram below to see the intervals of a chromatic scale, in the context of the guitar fretboard. We will be using **G** as the root note, the 3rd fret of our low **E** string:

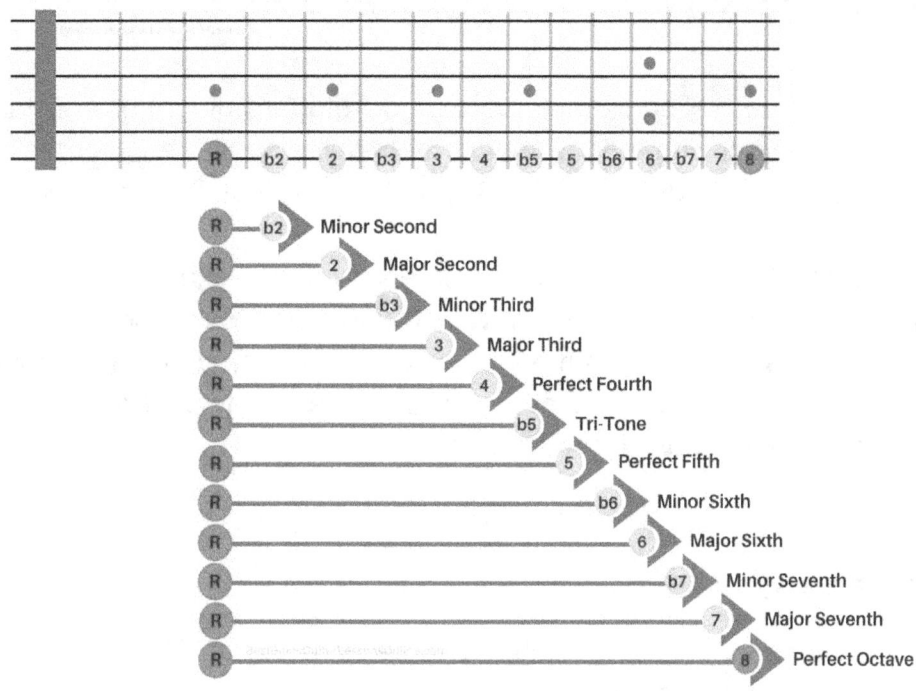

All of the intervals above use the root note **G**. The great thing about intervals is that the distance always remains the same no matter where you start from.

The first thing you need to know when trying to figure out an interval is what **root note** you are starting from. Once you have figured that out, all of the interval relationships will be the same as the chromatic scale above.

Let's say that you have the note **C** and you want to find the **Major Second** interval:

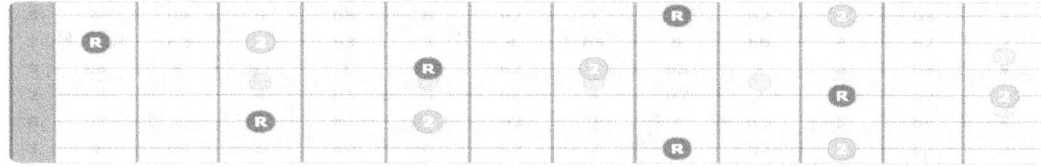

No matter which of the **C** roots that you start from on the fretboard, you will be able to find the Major second a whole step higher.

Internalizing Intervals with Popular Songs

Though it is easy to distinguish intervals on a fretboard diagram or in tablature, identifying and memorizing them with your ears takes some serious training. This is why using popular songs to remember your intervals can be *extremely* helpful.

Once you have internalized what certain intervals sound like, you will be able to recognize them with ease as you move through your scales or improvise later down the line. It is highly recommended to *play* these as you learn about them; use the **G** chromatic scale from earlier, or any note that you'd like, to play these intervals. See if you recognize the sounds!

Minor Second - Jaws

The minor second is the smallest interval in western music. The notes in a minor second are separated by a half-step.

One of the best pieces of music that represents the minor interval is the theme song from the movie *Jaws*. The opening notes in this theme song alternate between **E** and **F**, moving up a minor second, and repeating.

Major Second - Happy Birthday

A major second is the next interval in the series. It is the distance of one whole-step (or two half-steps).

Almost everyone and their mother knows about "Happy Birthday". The beauty of using the song to study intervals is that the very beginning of the song uses a major second. You can hear the major second as you move from the "py" syllable in "happy" to the word "birth".

Minor Third - Greensleeves

A minor third is made up of one-whole step and one half-step.

So many guitarists don't think they know the song "Greensleeves", though you might be surprised as to how popular this little Christmas tune is. The very first two notes in the song are a minor third apart.

If you don't know "Greensleeves", another good reference is the song "Hey Jude" by the Beatles. The interval is still a minor third, the difference is that it is descending rather than ascending.
One more quick reference for a minor third is the opening interval in the classic piece "Lullaby". The first two notes are the same, "Lul-a-" then the minor third occurs to get to the note on the syllable "by".

Major Third - When The Saints Go Marching In

Moving out of the darkness and into a much happier realm, we have the major third. A major third is made up of two whole-steps.

One of the best tunes to identify a major third is "When the Saints Go Marching In". The first two notes in the song, or the words "Oh" and "When", have a major third interval between them.

For a major third that is descending, you can make use of the first two notes in the popular spiritual piece, "Swing Low, Sweet Chariot".

Perfect Fourth - Amazing Grace

We have four different perfect intervals in music as we discussed earlier. As a reminder, these perfect intervals include:

- Perfect Fourths
- Perfect Fifths
- Perfect Unison
- Perfect Octave

Now as to *why* they are referred to as perfect would require some deep, historical analysis that would cloud the focus of this book. Instead, what is more important to remember is that the quality of fourths and fifths stay the same regardless of if they are in a major key or a minor key; major and minor scales both share perfect fourths, and perfect fifths.

A perfect fourth has a distance of two whole-steps and a half-step.

One of the best songs to use to remember the perfect fourth is "Amazing Grace". The first two notes in the song have a fourth interval between them. If you are looking for a descending fourth, we recommend checking out the Christmas classic, "O Come, All Ye Faithful". There is a descending fourth between the first two changing notes of the song.

Augmented 4th, Diminished 5th, Tritone - The Simpsons

Think back to earlier in this chapter when we discussed the idea of the *diminished* and *augmented* intervals. This next interval has three possible names: an augmented fourth, a diminished fifth, or a tritone. The typical shorthand for this interval is a tritone, but in the context of certain scales it will make sense to only refer to it as a diminished 5th, or augmented 4th.

This interval is the distance of three whole steps.

Identifying tritones is not very easy, as they have a dissonant sound. Luckily, we have a tritone in the beginning of one of the most famous television show theme songs of all time, *The Simpsons.* If you're a fan of musicals, the opening interval for the song "Maria" from the musical *West Side Story* is also a tritone.

Perfect Fifth - Twinkle, Twinkle, Little Star

The perfect fifth is the interval that people seem to internalize the fastest, as it is one of the strongest sounding intervals around; there's a lot of music history within this reasoning that involves fundamental overtones that go back to the beginning to music history itself. Perfect fifth intervals show up in all kinds of chords, from major to minor and beyond. No matter if you are in a major or minor key, your perfect fifth will always sound the same.

A perfect fifth consists of three whole-steps and one half-step.

Some of the most popular songs for identifying the perfect fifth interval are classic children's tunes: "Twinkle Twinkle Little Star"; "Alphabet Song"; or "Baa Baa Black Sheep". All of these songs have the same melody and they contain the jump of a perfect fifth within the first notes. The opening interval for the theme from *Star Wars*, sometimes called "Luke's Theme," is a perfect fifth as well.

For descending perfect fifths, we would highly recommend checking out the theme song from *The Flintstones.* A descending perfect fifth can be found in the first two notes of the song.

Minor Sixth - The Entertainer

A minor sixth might just be the hardest interval to identify next to the tritone, as it isn't commonly used. The interval is made up of four whole-steps. It is one half-step bigger than a perfect fifth.

One of the best songs to grasp the minor sixth interval with is the Scott Joplin classic, "The Entertainer". It is probably one of the most played piano songs around. The very beginning of the tune moves up a minor sixth and down a minor sixth several times during the main recurring theme.

For a more modern approach to the minor sixth, we recommend looking at the song "We Are Young" by the band Fun. A minor sixth can be found in the chorus when he sings "Fire" and "Brighter".

Major Sixth - My Bonnie Lies Over The Ocean

The major sixth interval is composed of four whole-steps and one half-step. People often use the first two notes of the chimes in the *NBC* jingle to find the major sixth: the notes that reflect the part "N-B" are a major sixth.

Another popular piece of music that is associated with the major sixth is the traditional Scottish piece, "My Bonnie Lies Over The Ocean". Moving from "My" to "Bon", we can hear the major sixth interval.

If you're looking for a descending major sixth, look no further than the descending major sixth found in the beginning of the spiritual, "Nobody Knows the Trouble I've Seen". The descending major sixth is found in the first two notes of the song from the syllable "No" to the syllable "bod".

Minor Seventh - Somewhere (*West Side Story*)

Two intervals that often get mixed up are minor seventh and major sevenths, as they are very far from the root, though very close to the octave. This interval is used often in jazz to outline chord changes. The notes in a minor seventh interval is five whole-steps apart.

We can hear a minor seventh in the song "Somewhere" from *West Side Story*. The minor seventh is found at the beginning of the song from the word "There's" to the word "a".

Major Seventh - Take On Me

The largest interval before the octave is the famed major seventh! The major seventh is just one half-step below the octave and is made up of five whole-steps and a half-step. One of the best songs to grasp the major seventh with is the song "Take On Me" from the 80s one-hit-wonder, A-Ha.

The first two words at the start of the chorus use a major second as he moves from "Take" to "On".

Hopefully these reference songs will help your understanding of intervals. Hearing and recognizing intervals naturally will help tremendously as you progress through your scales. You'll be able to make better sense of sounds within different scales, which will allow you to improvise with ease down the line. To quiz yourself on identifying the sound of intervals, you can search the web for "interval quiz", or visit musictheory.net.

Chapter 4 - Understanding Keys

Now that we have a better understanding of **intervals**, let's move on and talk about another fundamental concept in scales, and that is the concept of **"key"**.

The idea of a key is a bit of an abstract one, to say the least, and it can seem fairly mystifying to most. As you begin to dive deeper into the world of keys, the concept will become far clearer. We highly recommend coming back to this lesson a few times throughout the book to reset your foundation.

Now onto the question,

What is a key?

A **key** in music is essentially the scale that a piece of music revolves around. That scale can either be **major** or **minor**. A piece of music that is in a **major key** will use a **major scale** and a piece of music that is in a **minor key** will use a **minor scale.**

Major Keys
Let's say that you have a song in the key of C major. The song will ultimately revolve around the notes that are present within the C major scale:

C-D-E-F-G-A-B-C

It is important to know that music often uses notes that are outside of the song's key for colorful effects; for example, if you inserted a **D#** in the scale above between the **D** and **E**, it would be out of the key, but it would add some flavor! Still, the song would remain in the key of C because the song's fundamentals—melody, chord structure, bassline—would still reflect the C major scale.

A song that is in G major, for example, will use the notes of the G major scale:

G-A-B-C-D-E-F#-G

Once again, if we were to add a note outside of the scale we would be adding color, but the song would remain in the key of G Major. For example, inserting a **C#** between the **C** and **D** would create a fun, bluesy sound. Try adding some colorful notes of your own!

Minor Keys
In the same way, a piece of music that is in a minor key will revolve around what is called the **natural minor scale**.

Let's say that we have a song in the key of D minor.

The song will ultimately revolve around the notes that are present within the D minor scale:

D-E-F-G-A-Bb-C

Minor scales have a very dramatic sound as it is. Adding colorful notes outside of the key is sometimes tricky. Try inserting a **C#** between the **C** and **D** for this scale.

The takeaway here is that a major or minor scale acts to serve the key to a piece of music. It is the broth of the soup, so to speak. Additional notes outside of the key add intrigue and flavor, but the broth is still the fundamental ingredient.

Understanding the Root

The root note, otherwise known as the **tonic**, will act as the fundamental note that the key circles around. The root note in a key is similar to the root note in a chord.

Let's say that we are working in the key of C major. In that case, the root note or tonic would be **C**. The root of the G major scale would be **G**, the root of the E minor scale would be **E**, and so on.

It's best to think of the tonic or the root as a sort of home base. Your key can bring you all over the world through ups and downs in a roller coaster of emotion (dramatic, huh?). The beauty is that it will eventually bring you back down to Earth where you feel at home.

Most music, especially popular western music, constantly pulls the listener's ear toward the tonic. This is a basic songwriting technique that leans on our interest in resolution. You may have noticed this type of motion as you're learning songs on the guitar; things always seem to come back to the root.

When you move up and down in a key and away from the tonic, you create interest for the listener. Eventually it comes back down to let the listener know that the musical phrase, or the song is coming to an end.

Notes Outside of The Key

As we mentioned before, we will sometimes have notes in a song that are *outside of the song's key*. While many people use outside notes when writing pieces of music, the majority of notes will center around the notes of the key, as well as the tonic.

When outside notes are used **improperly**, it can create a very unpleasant sound and throw off the whole tonality of the piece of music.

As you become more familiar with scales, you will be able to learn how to use outside notes without them sounding unpleasant or throwing off the key center. Creating interesting sounds through notes outside the key has been a practice of music writing for centuries. Even now, there are many genres of music where having outside notes can be beneficial, often blues and jazz. It is often that we find outside notes in heavy metal or hard rock riffs too.

How Many Keys Are In Music?

As we have already learned, there are 12 notes found in western music, each of which can be the root of a scale.

Most theory beginners will say there are only twelve major keys, and twelve minor keys; 24 total keys. However, the magic number is actually **30**. This is because of our enharmonic equivalents, which we defined earlier as two notes that sound the same but are written differently.

For example, the keys of F# major and Gb major use the same notes. The only difference is how we write out those scales.

The Gb major scale uses the notes

Gb-Ab-Bb-Cb-Db-Eb-F

While the F# major scale uses the notes

F#-G#-A#-B-C#-D#-E#

These are enharmonic equivalents. There are only 2 other keys that share this phenomenon where the whole scale will sound the same, but be spelled differently: Db Major=C# Major, and Cb Major=B Major. Don't get too concerned about this though; this is an advanced concept that we will explore later in the book, and all other keys do *not* concern this.

An Exercise in Understanding the Tonic

Pick a song to listen to. Can you find "home base"?

As you listen to that song, try to actively pay attention to the concept of the root as we discussed above and listen for where you believe the "resolution" of the song lies. Of course, there might be plenty of points of resolution throughout a song, though often, we find resolution at the end.

A majority of songs finish on the tonic of the key to let the listener know that the song has come to an end. This is because ending on the tonic is very natural and expected. Artists will sometimes use that expectation of a resolution to manipulate the emotional direction of the song, which can be very exciting to hear. This is resolving **deceptively**, meaning the root note won't be given to the listener, but instead a substitution will be made that gives us a certain feeling.

Of course, there are no hard and fast rules and many songwriters leave the ends of their songs unresolved for a certain effect.

It can be argued that we have a natural sense of tonality, though, which makes us yearn for the tonic.

As we move through the scales in our next chapters, you will become more aware of this concept.

Chapter 5 - The Major Scale

Ah yes, the major scale.

The mother of all scales!

Pretty much all of the scales, intervals, chords, and modes that we use in western music can be derived from the major scale. When it comes to making music, we use the major scale as a reference very often.

Having an idea of the major scale can give you a sense of what it is that you are playing on the guitar, whether you are playing rhythm or lead. Plus, playing all of your major scales is **excellent** for warming up.

The Sound of the Major Scale

Let's take a second and think back to *The Sound of Music.* One of its most popular songs goes something like this:

"Do, re, mi, fa, so, la, ti do".

You know the song, right? Or at the very least, you've probably heard those words in that order somewhere before. Well that, my friends, is the major scale. It is extremely important that you know what it sounds like so that you can recognize it while you are playing it.

The major scale is constructed with seven different notes. The first note is the root (**1**) and moves on through a series of numbers until you reach the octave, a higher version of the root, which is **8**. That series looks something like this:

1-2-3-4-5-6-7-8

The octave (**8**), as we know, is the same note as the root, though eight notes higher. This means that once we reach the **8**, we could start the scale all over again.

The Major Scale Formula

In order to construct a major scale correctly, we need to have the right pattern of whole steps and half steps. The pattern for constructing a major scale goes like this:

W-W-H-W-W-W-H

- The "W" stands for "Whole-Step" and is equal to two frets
- The "H" stands for "Half-Step" and is equal to one fret

The major scale can be constructed on any note you want, as long as it follows this formula.

As an example, let's begin our major scale on the note **G**. We will begin our major scale on the **G** that is on the third fret of the sixth (low E) string. From **G**, move up a **whole step** to the note **A**; a **whole step** up to the note **B**; a **half step** up to the note C; a **whole step** up to the note **D**; a **whole step** up to the note **E**; a **whole step** up to the note **F#**, and finally we resolve up one **half step** to the octave **G**.

The notes of the **G** major scale are:

G-A-B-C-D-E-F#-G

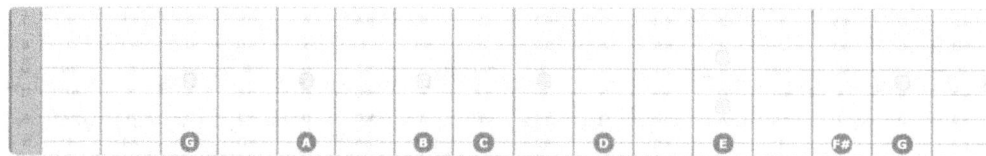

Play through this series a couple of times until you have a better understanding of how the G Major scale sounds.

Moveable Major Scale Patterns

While it is helpful to know the major scale moving up one string, you will more often play your major scale using **movable major scale patterns**.

Let's take the G Major scale again. We will still start on the **G** that is on the third fret of the low E stringas we did before, though we will move up through different strings rather than staying on the low E string. This will be a *two-octave* scale, so it will be twice as long as our G scale that we just played on one string.

The beauty of these movable patterns is that you can shift them up or down on the fretboard to play a different major scale. We'll get there soon, but for now, let's take a look at the movable **G Major Scale pattern**:

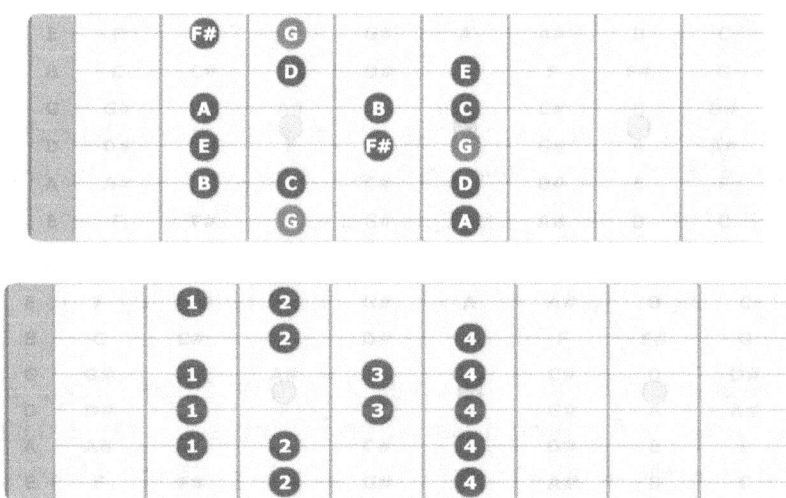

The diagram on top shows the notes in the scale while the diagram on the bottom shows your finger positioning as you move up the scale.

- **1** = Index Finger
- **2** = Middle Finger
- **3** = Ring Finger
- **4** = Pinky

Moving This Scale to a Different Key

Now let's move the entire G Major scale that we have right here up two frets so that our root (**1**) is **A**. The pattern will stay exactly the same, though all of the notes will be shifted two frets up.

If the root note is **G**, you have a **G** major scale. Then therefore if the root note is **A**, you have an **A** major scale. Use the same fingerings that we had above as well; this fingering will be used for any major scale starting on the low E string.

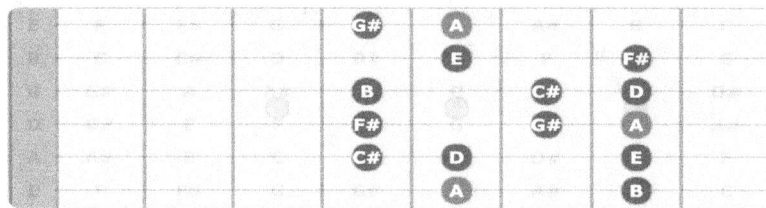

When it comes down to it, these major scale patterns can also be defined as **two-octave patterns**, as they span two octaves. Once you reach the first octave from the root, you start the scale all over again, just an octave higher.

There are a few different ways in which you can practice this scale:

- Start by practicing your scale up and down on single strings. Pick a note to start on and use the **Whole-Half Step Formula.** Be intent in listening to the scale as you move up and down and sing the notes out loud if you can.
- Next, practice your **two-octave** G major scale pattern, starting from the third fret on the low **E** string, both in ascending and descending. Make sure to use a metronome and start slow while increasing your speed as you get more comfortable. The goal here is to play every note with a good sound and to stay in time.
- Lastly, move your major scale shape pattern to different keys on the low E string. Start with **G** major, then move up a fret each time you start over to play a new scale; make sure you are identifying which scale you're playing by finding out your starting note, or root. You could also try starting on notes before **G** on the low E string.

The Five Major Scale CAGED Positions

The beauty of the major scale is that once you know how to play it in one position, you can easily begin to move it up and down the neck of the guitar. This is where the five **CAGED** shapes come in handy.

The CAGED shapes come from the CAGED system, which essentially gives guitarists a more logical overview of the fretboard.

C-A-G-E-D stands for **C** shape, **A** shape, **G** shape, **E** shape, and **D** shape. These shapes span the entire length of the fretboard. These shapes are also referred to as "positions". This system makes it easier to understand the location of scales and chord shapes, as well as triads, licks, and arpeggios on the guitar.
We're going to start by looking at the key of **G** major, as it is one of the most popular major scales on the guitar.

All of the CAGED shapes that we are going to look at will use the G major scale. With that said, it is important to note that the scale shapes we are going to look at will apply to all other major keys as well, as the shapes are meant to be moved up and down the length of the fretboard.

For example, if you move any of the CAGED shapes using the G major scale up two frets, you will have the A major scale.

Every scale shape correlates to a chord shape so that you can easily identify each scale. As you move through the scale diagrams below, you will see the chord shape (displayed with blue and red dots) that sits within the scale shape.

Take a look at the diagrams below and begin playing each scale shape by starting at the lowest root note, which is the red note labeled with an "R". Play the scale all the way up to the highest note on the high **E** string before coming back down to the lowest note on the low **E** string, then back up to the first root that you started with.

G Major Scale - E Shape / Position 1

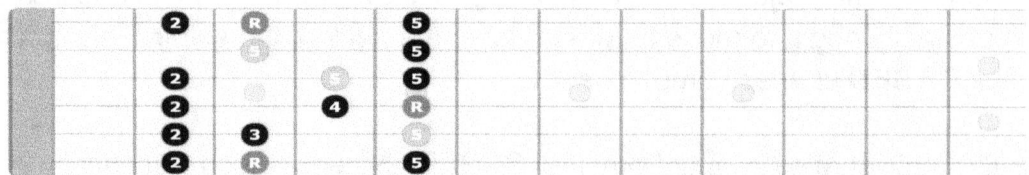

G Major Scale - D Shape / Position 2

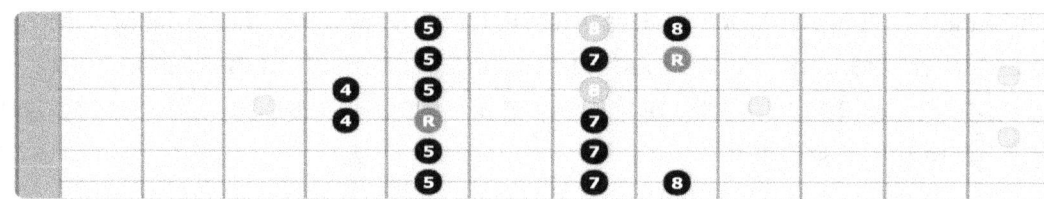

G Major Scale - C Shape / Position 3

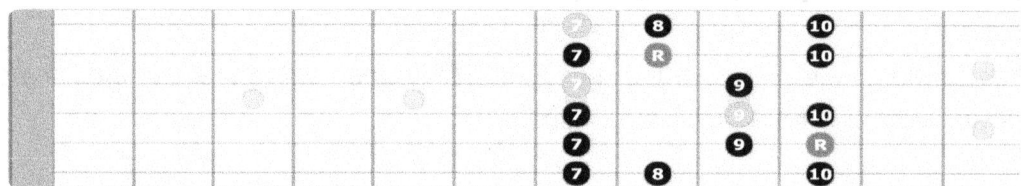

G Major Scale - A Shape / Position 4

G Major Scale - G Shape / Position 5

Practicing Scale Shapes

Of course, knowing these scale shapes isn't enough. You must also know how to practice them.

We highly recommend practicing these scales with a pick using an alternate picking method; meaning you start with a downstroke, then upstroke, down, up, down, up, etc. We also recommend using a metronome once the patterns are comfortable. When playing with a metronome, start with the click on a slow BPM, like 90 or less, and listen to how the notes that you're playing align with the click of the metronome. This type of focused practice is used by professional musicians often; if it isn't in time, it doesn't count!

Each note should sound crisp and clear; watch out for fret buzz when you're using that pinky, for example. You will want to visualize every chord shape while you are playing the scale so that you have a good understanding of the shape before you move on to the next one. This will require some time and patience, though once you have it under your belt, you will be one step closer to scale success!

Three Notes Per String Major Scale Patterns

While the CAGED system is one of the most useful systems for learning about guitar scales and chords, there is another system out there that is just as efficient. That system is called the...

Three Notes Per String System

The three notes per string system is just as the name implies. The idea here is that you play three notes per string across the fretboard in different positions. As you move up the scale, you don't have to move from three notes on one string to two notes on the next string and back, like in the CAGED system.

The three notes per string system is a bit more uniform, which is helpful for many guitarists since it helps to simplify the number of notes played on each string.

Of course, the *downside* to the three notes per string system is that it requires a bit more flexibility. Some of the notes in the three notes per string system are four frets apart. If you don't have adequate flexibility, or your fingers aren't long enough, you may find these patterns quite difficult to play.

Compared to the CAGED patterns, you have a bit more patterns to learn here too. In total, we have **seven** patterns in this system.

This system is by no means the *best* system, though we felt it was important to include, as there are many guitarists who find it more effective. Let's take a look at some of the three notes per string major scale positions.

The following scales are in the key of F Major, which is the widest part of the fretboard so make sure you stretch your hand out before playing this one. You can use these same patterns on different roots up and down the fretboard. Remember that each position is played in an ascending and descending fashion.

If you run into a series of notes that span five frets, it is recommended that you use your index finger to hit the first note, your middle finger to hit the second note, and your pinky to hit the third note.

Practice with a metronome!

Position 1

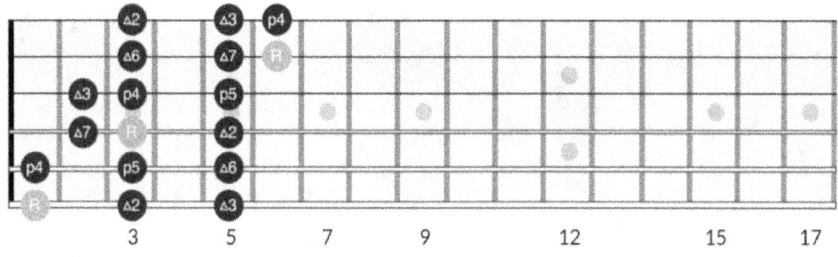

Postion 2

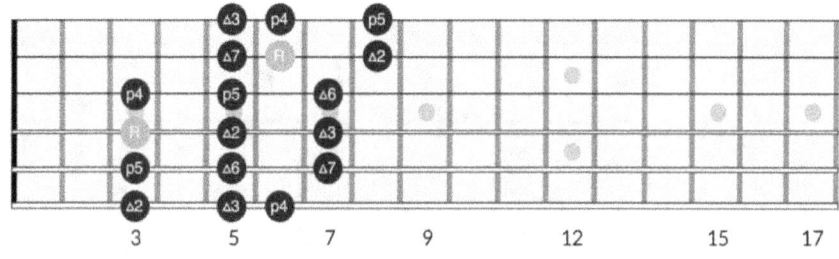

Position 3

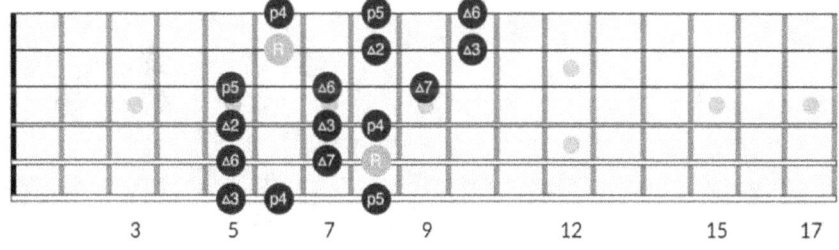

Position 4

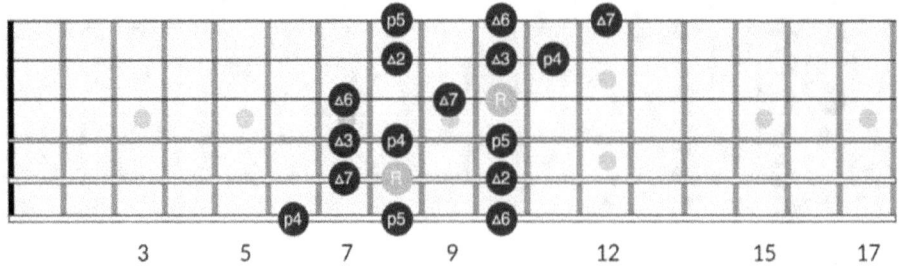

Position 5

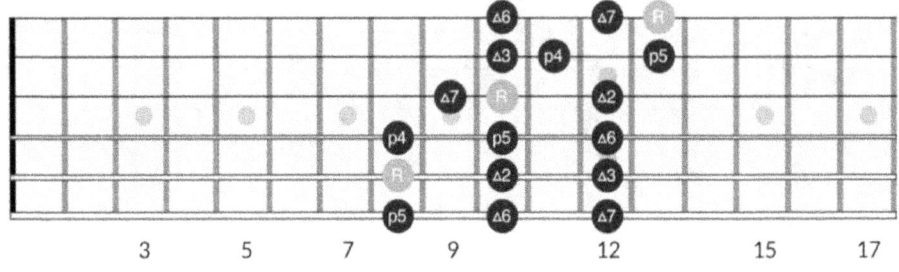

Position 6

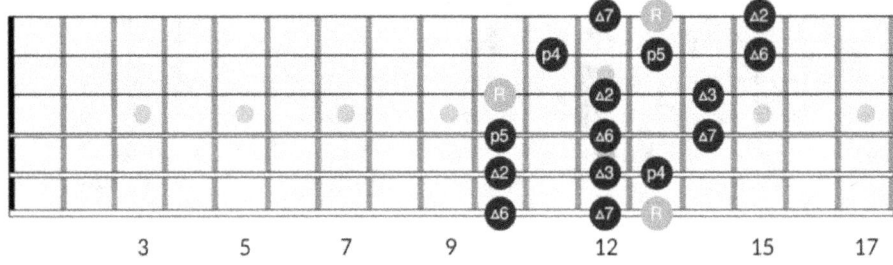

Position 7

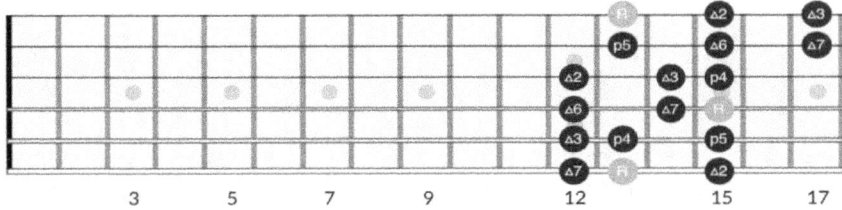

The three notes per string major scale patterns is simply another tool that you can use to navigate the notes on the fretboard. When you combine these patterns with the popular CAGED patterns, the guitar opens up.

Next, let's move into the realm of minor scales.

Chapter 6 - The Minor Scale

Whenever most guitarists play over songs that are in minor keys, they tend to exclusively use the pentatonic scale, which we will get into later. The problem with the pentatonic scale is that it will always sound somewhat bluesy or rock-y.

This is why we like to use the minor scale. There are some songs out there that are just asking for a more straightforward approach to a melody, which is exactly where the minor scale can be helpful.

There are three main types of minor scales out there:

- **Natural Minor Scale**
- **Harmonic Minor Scale**
- **Melodic Minor Scale**

The Minor Scale Formula

The natural minor scale is very common and has a scale formula that looks like this:

1-2-b3-4-5-b6-b7-8

If we compare that scale to the major scale, which we went over in the last chapter, that looks like this: **1-2-3-4-5-6-7-8**, we can see that the minor scale has a minor third, a minor sixth, and a minor seventh.

If you begin on your root note and build a natural minor scale pattern using whole and half-steps, you end up with a pattern that looks like this:

Whole-Half-Whole-Whole-Half-Whole-Whole

Understanding Relative Minor Scales

We can think of the natural minor scale as a **relative minor scale** too.

This is because every major scale has a minor scale that shares the same exact notes, which we refer to as the **relative minor**. Take any major scale and move up to the sixth scale degree; make that note your new root. From that sixth degree, our new root, play seven notes in an ascending order to get your relative minor scale.
So essentially, you have a major scale and its relative minor scale in the same spot, though you can also think of it as a natural minor scale with a relative major. This can sometimes be confusing, but the important part to remember is that a major and relative minor share the exact same notes.

The C Major scale, for example, has these notes:

C-D-E-F-G-A-B-C

If we go up to the sixth scale degree, we get to the note A. This is our new root for the relative minor. Therefore, the A natural minor scale shares the same notes as the C major scale, though starts on **A**:

A-B-C-D-E-F-G

Let's take the same approach to the G Major scale now.

The G Major scale looks like this:

G-A-B-C-D-E-F#-G

The 6th scale degree is E, so the E natural minor scale is the relative minor of the G major scale; it shares the same notes, though is played starting on **E**:

E-F#-G-A-B-C-D-E

Here is what the A natural minor scale looks like starting on the low **E** string:

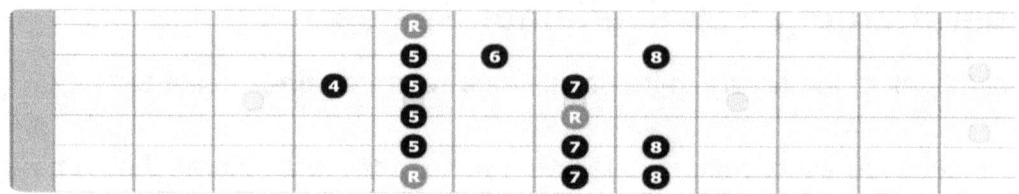

Just like our major scales, we can move this shape around to find any minor scale on the low E string. So if you want to play the B natural minor scale, for example, all you would have to do is shift this scale **up** a whole-step or two frets. If you want to play the G natural minor scale, for example, you would shift it **down** by a whole-step, or two frets.

Now let's take a look at the five natural minor scale shapes:

A Minor Scale - Position 1

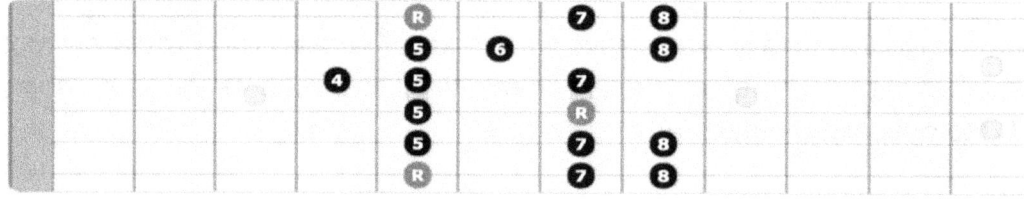

A Minor Scale - Position 2

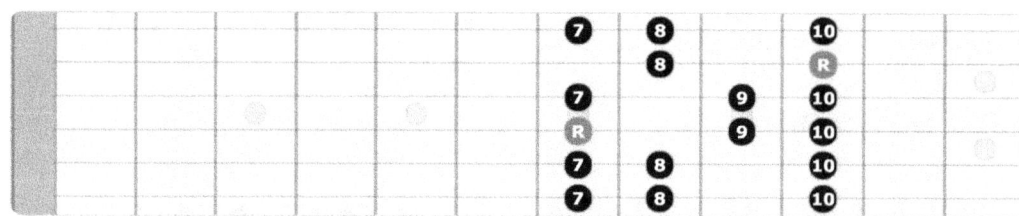

A Minor Scale - Position 3

A Minor Scale - Position 4

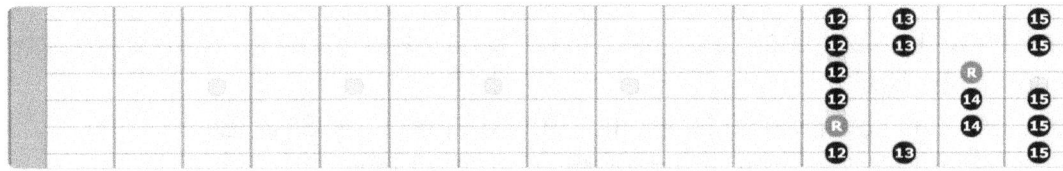

A Minor Scale - Position 5

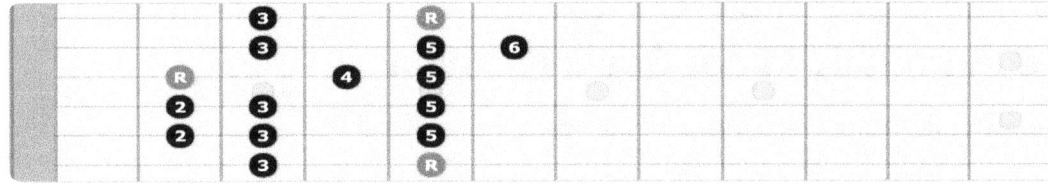

When practicing these scales, treat them like you would the major scale.

Practice these scales using an alternate picking method; down, up, down, up, down, etc. Use a metronome as well and start slowly so that you make sure that you are hitting every note perfectly before moving on.

The Harmonic Minor Scale

Now that you have a better understanding of natural minor scale, let's implement the **harmonic minor scale**. We often see the harmonic minor scale used in horror-film music, Spanish flamenco, gypsy jazz, and neo-classical music.

With that said, it is *also* a very popular scale in rock genres, as it moves a bit outside of the natural minor scale. It provides us with sounds that conjure up a bit of Middle Eastern spice and feel. Essentially, the harmonic minor scale can be used to make things interesting.

To hear real-life examples of the harmonic minor scale, we recommend listening to guitarists such as Joe Satriani or John Petrucci, as they use the harmonic natural scale quite often when they are soloing. The harmonic minor scale is used in many well-known pieces of music:

Classical: "Toccata and Fugue in D minor" by Johann S. Bach; "Hungarian Dance" by Johannes Brahms
Pop: "Believer" by Imagine Dragons; "Bury a Friend" by Billie Eilish
Soundtrack: *Prelude* from the soundtrack to the movie *Psycho*.

Knowing the harmonic minor scale can add a bit of flavor to your solos and is great for playing over minor chords or dominant seventh chords.

The Harmonic Minor Scale Formula

The formula for the harmonic minor scale looks like this:

1-2-b3-4-5-b6-7-8
When compared to the major scale, the harmonic minor scale has a lowered third and sixth. The difference between the harmonic minor scale and the natural minor scale is that raised seventh scale degree; this is a very distinctive sound, which gives the harmonic minor scale its flair.

The pattern of the harmonic minor scale looks like this:

Whole-Half-Whole-Whole-Half-(Whole + Half)-Half

Here is what an A Harmonic minor scale looks like starting on the low **E** string:

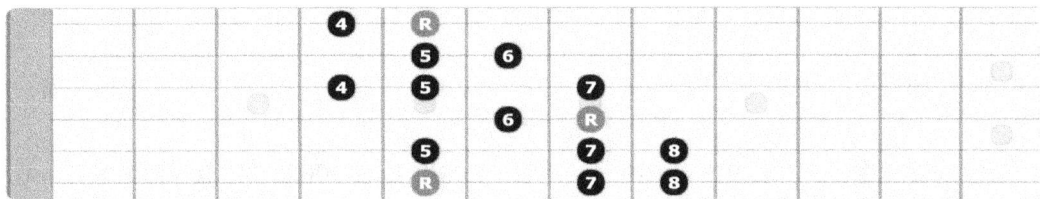

You can practice this scale in the same manner as the natural minor scale by using a metronome and moving in ascending and descending order, listening to your precision with the metronome.

When Do We Use The Harmonic Minor Scale?

The harmonic minor scale is often played over a minor chord or a song that is in a minor key. Let's say that you are playing over a song that is in E minor. Rather than using the natural minor scale, try out the harmonic minor to add a bit of spice to your sound.

It is also worth noting that the harmonic minor scale can work really well over dominant seventh chords too.

A dominant seven chord–if you use roman numerals, would be notated as V7 and is built on the fifth degree of a major or minor scale.

If you are in the key of E minor, for example, the dominant seven chord would be **B7**, since **B** is the fifth scale degree in the E minor scale. A **B7** chord contains that major seventh within the harmonic minor scale.

You could also play the E natural minor scale for the majority of the tune and then switch into the E harmonic minor scale whenever the **B7** came around.

The Melodic Minor Scale

The melodic minor scale is often referred to as the "minor jazz scale". It is a must-know scale for any guitarist who wants to get into playing jazz.

The formula for the melodic minor scale is as follows:

1-2-b3-4-5-6-7

The difference between the melodic minor scale and the harmonic minor scale is that the melodic minor scale uses a raised sixth degree.
Traditionally, the melodic minor scale has this pattern when ascending, but when descending the notes reflect the natural minor scale. However, this is a bigger deal when composing classical music and dealing with harmony.

It is important to understand that the melodic scale creates tension when it is played over a minor seventh chord, as it has a major seventh present in it.

This is why jazz players who play with the melodic minor scale know how to resolve their guitar lines properly to get rid of that tension.

Here is what the A Melodic Minor Scale looks like:

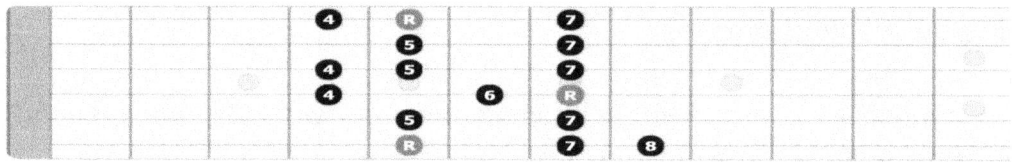

Chapter 7 - The Pentatonic Scale

Now that we know the basics of major scales and minor scales, we are going to move forward and talk about major and minor pentatonic scales. We will also discuss where you can use these scales and why they make such excellent shortcuts for guitarists!

The pentatonic scale contains only five notes, which is how the name was derived.

Penta = five
Tonic = tones

There are both major and minor pentatonic scales. Pentatonic scales are somewhat of a shortcut for guitarists learning scales.

- The major pentatonic scale can be played over just about any major chord or dominant chord without having the feeling of dissonance.
- The minor pentatonic scale can be played over just about any minor chord without having the feeling of dissonance.
- There are often times where both scales can be played over a chord, especially when you are playing blues or rock music.

Sounds pretty awesome, right?

This is precisely what makes the pentatonic scale such a popular scale choice for guitarists in many styles!

Major and Minor Pentatonic Scale Formulas

Remember the scale degree patterns that we talked about earlier?

Well, the pentatonic scale uses that too!

Here are the formulas for the major and minor pentatonic scales:

Minor Pentatonic - 1-b3-4-5-b7-8

Major Pentatonic - 1-2-3-5-6-8

Let's say that you were trying to find the notes of the A minor pentatonic scale. To do so, you could simply apply the corresponding scale formula to the scale of A minor:

A Minor - A-B-C-D-E-F-G-A
A Minor Pentatonic - A-C-D-E-G

If you look above, you can see that we have only used the first, third, fourth, fifth, and seventh notes from the A minor scale to get the **five notes** of the minor pentatonic scale.

If you were to try and find the major pentatonic scale, the process is almost identical. The notes we use from the A major scale are the first, second, third, fifth, and sixth. You could also look at it this way: all you have to do is get rid of the fourth and seventh scale degrees from the major scale.

A Major - A-B-C#-D-E-F#-G#-A
A Major Pentatonic - A-B-C#-E-F#-A

Essentially, you just end up with the A major scale without the **D** and **G#**!

This formula can be used for all major and minor pentatonic scales no matter what the root of the scale is. Understanding this formula will help you to have a deeper understanding of the scale, rather than just using pattern memorization techniques.

Pentatonic Patterns

While it is incredibly important to have an understanding of the pentatonic formula, you will also want to learn the box patterns for the different pentatonic scales, as they can be linked to the CAGED system, which we discussed earlier.

The great thing about these pentatonic patterns is that they can be moved up and down the fretboard with ease.

To start, here are the minor pentatonic shaped patterns and the intervals within them. The root note positions match the root note positions of the CAGED shape patterns (indicated with the white circles in each of these diagrams):

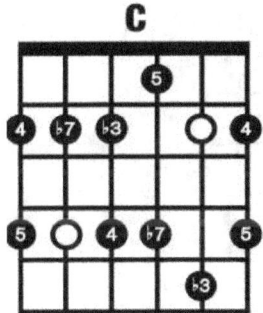
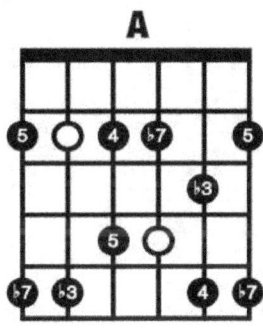
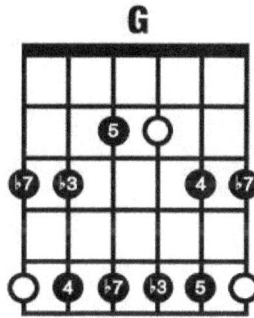
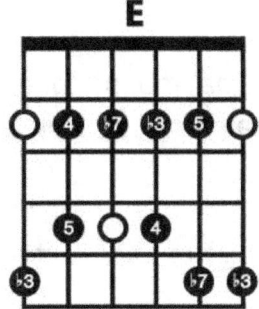
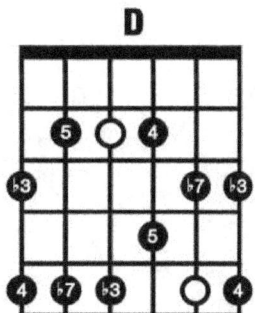

The same thing goes for the major pentatonic scale. The pattern found on these scales differs from the minor pentatonic scale, though the root positions are exactly the same. One of the best ways to remember these patterns is by keeping an eye on the root note. Once you have a good idea of where the roots are, reading the scale shapes will become much easier.

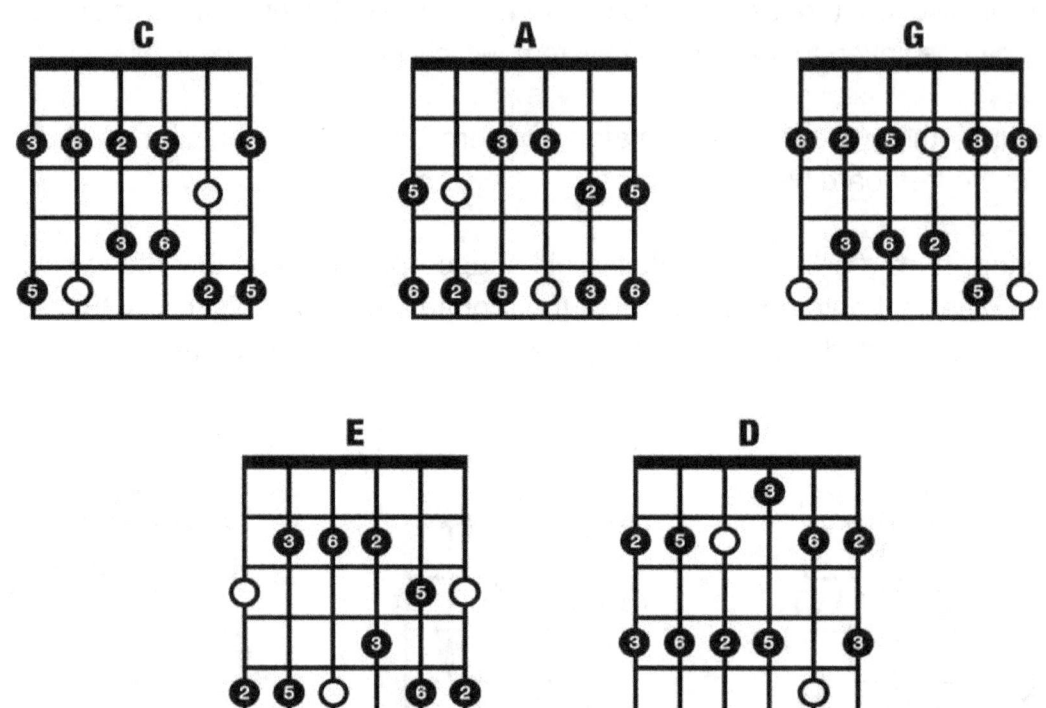

Playing Over Major Chords

When you are playing over a major chord, the major pentatonic scale serves as a great choice for improvisation. The major pentatonic scale has a comforting sound and is useful for making quick melodic hooks.

Let's say you have a C Major chord, the C Major pentatonic scale would of course be one of your options.

Now, this isn't to say the major pentatonic is your only correct scale. Try playing the C minor pentatonic scale over the major chord. It will get you a bluesy sound because of the way the notes sit over a major chord; the minor pentatonic scale uses a **b3** (minor third) and a b7 (minor seventh) interval, while the major chord has a major third which is more acceptable to the ear since a major triad also has no seventh for it to "rub against".

Playing Over Minor Chords

When you are playing over a minor chord, the minor pentatonic scale is a great option.

Let's say you have an A minor chord; you could use the A minor pentatonic scale.

Playing Over Dominant Chords

When playing over a dominant chord, you can use both major or minor pentatonic scales. Like before, though, you need to be very cautious of the minor third whenever you are using the minor pentatonic scale.

Let's say you have a C7 chord. There are many things to consider if you are playing over it; whether you are improvising, composing a melody, or just experimenting. The C Major pentatonic and the C minor pentatonic can both work, but there are considerations.

Dominant chords use major thirds and minor sevenths. The minor pentatonic uses a minor third, which could create dissonance (a crunchy sound that can sometimes be undesirable) with the major third of the chord. On the other hand, the minor pentatonic scale contains the minor seventh, which will sound great since it matches the minor 7th in the chord.

The major pentatonic scale is a good choice because it does not have any clashing notes in it. Though, the 6th in the major pentatonic does create some friction because it is only a half-step from the minor 7th in the dominant chord.

Once you have the major and minor pentatonic scales down, you are pretty much ready to play the blues. Of course, you can take it one step further with the Blues scale!

The Blues Scale

The blues scale finds its home in rock, country, and of course, blues. It is a six-note scale that adds one chromatic note to the minor pentatonic scale. This additional note is often referred to as the "blue note", and it is exactly what provides the blues scale with that legendary bluesy sound that great guitarists like Eric Clapton, Jimi Hendrix, B.B. King and countless others use with great taste.

Getting to know the blues scale will help you to improvise over a wide variety of musical styles and chord progressions, including driving rock and roll tunes, jazz standards, or 12 bar blues progressions.

Similar to the major and minor pentatonic scales, the blues scale can be played in either major or minor. To make it easy, we will solely focus on the minor blues scale in this little lesson, as it is one of the most popular blues scales around.

The notes in the A minor blues scale are as follows:

A-C-D-D#-E-G-A

Just like any scale on the guitar, you can move this scale around to any root, as the intervals that make up the minor blues scales are the same in every single key!

The whole and half-step pattern is tricky in the blues scale because there's so much distance between the notes:

(Whole + Half)-Whole-Half-Half-(Whole + Half)-Whole

An alternative to the whole and half-step pattern is to use our scale degrees from earlier.

1-b3-4-#4-5-b7

The fourth note in the pattern above is the blue note, which is D# in this instance. As you walk your fingers up chromatically from the **D,** to the **D#**, to the **E**, you get this awesome blues sound that truly distinguishes the scale from all the others.

As with all of the other scales that we have looked at thus far, the A minor blues scale has a few different positions. Here they are up and down the neck (the numbers shown tell you which fingers to use (1=pointer; 2=middle; 3=ring; 4=pinky):

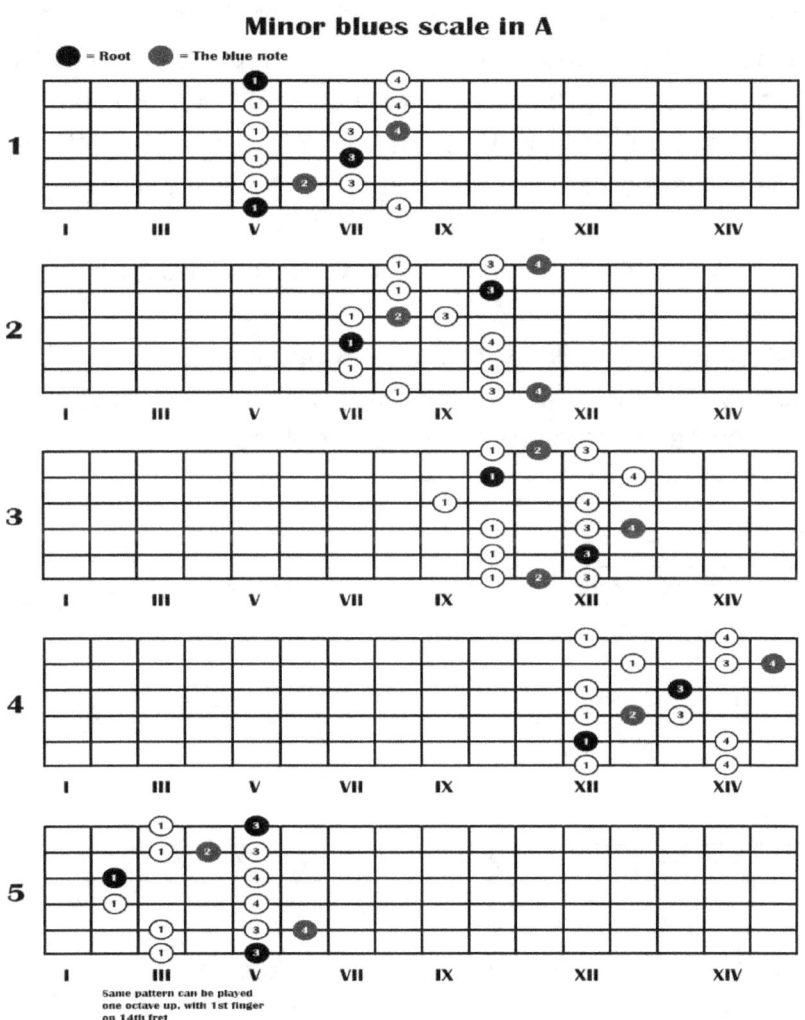

Playing 12 Bar Blues

One of the best ways to practice the blues scale is by playing the blues! Plus, it's fun to do something applicable once in a while rather than just practicing scales over and over again.

Of course, it *is* necessary to have a good idea of the scales, so make sure to spend a bit of time going through each position until you feel comfortable with them, just like we've done with the other scales in the book thus far.

The blues scale sounds wonderful on a variety of different chord progressions, though there is no question that it sounds best when played over 12 bar blues. The traditional 12 bar blues progression contains three chords, which are the 1, 4, and 5 (or roman numerals: **I**, **IV**, and **V**) of any given scale. These chords are almost always dominant 7th chords, which is integral to the blues sound.

In the A minor blues scale, for example, those chords would be **A7**, **D7**, and **E7**.

When you play the 12 bar blues, you will probably recognize it right off the bat. This is because you've heard it a million times in blues, country, and rock and roll music. Here is the basic structure of the 12 bar blues:

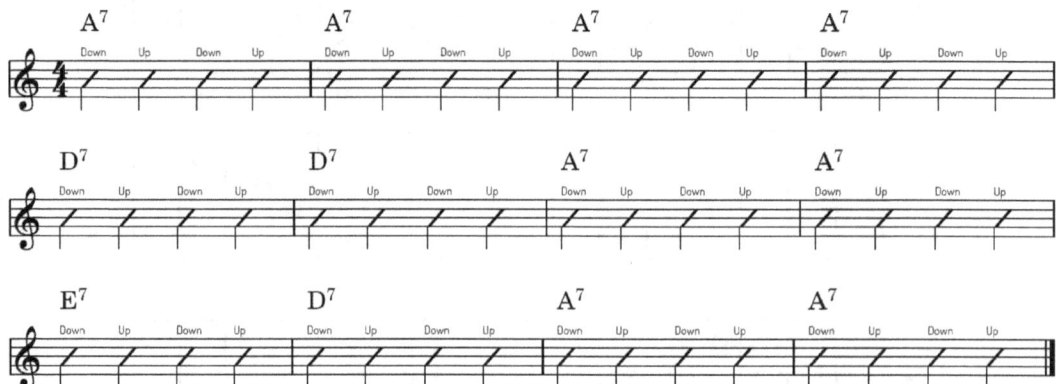

Pay close attention to the strumming pattern, marked as up and down through the music. Blues music has a "swing feel" so you should play these chords in a shuffle rhythm. If you don't know what a shuffle rhythm is, we would highly recommend looking it up before you get started to get the feel right. Take a listen to some classic blues riffs like "Roadhouse Blues", "Rocky Mountain Way", or "Bad to the Bone"; try to mimic the rhythm in these songs when playing through this chord progression.

Once you feel confident with your blues scales and the 12 bar blues structure, find a looping 12 bar A minor blues accompaniment (a quick YouTube search will do just fine) and practice playing your A minor blues scale in each of the five positions over it.

Start out by treating the notes on each string as one phrase. Once you are feeling comfortable with that, you can try breaking your scale up into three or four-note phrases that span across the strings. Eventually, you will feel comfortable enough to improvise or write out some lead parts using the blues scale.

Chapter 8 - Major Modes

Up until now, we've mostly learned about **parent scales.**

I say mostly because we *did* touch on the pentatonic and blues scales, which we are not considering as parent scales. The other scales, however, namely the major and minor scales, are **parent** scales.

A parent scale can be defined as a seven-note device that can be a reference **mode** for each of the seven notes present. If you play a C Major scale, for example, you will produce seven possible modes from it (one for each of the notes in the scale).

So what exactly is a mode?

The best way to think about a mode is by considering the fact that they share the same notes as their parent scale, though because of each mode's starting place in the scale, they use **different intervals.**

If you play a C Major scale starting and ending with C, for example, you of course get a regular C Major scale. However, if you played the notes of a C Major scale starting on D, you get one of the modes and it would look like this:

D-E-F-G-A-B-C-D

This particular mode is called the **D Dorian mode** and it has a very distinct sound when played on the guitar; it is often used in funk and soul music. When compared side by side with C Major here is how the intervals look:

- **C Major** - 1-2-3-4-5-6-7
- **D Dorian** - 1-2-b3-4-5-6-b7

Now, though the parent scale and the mode share the same notes, they can be used to improvise or solo over different chords or chord progressions. Of course, this still may seem a bit difficult to understand, especially if you are brand new to the idea of modes. We're hoping that it will become crystal clear after this lesson!

Theory is sometimes harder to grasp when looking at it on paper. As you read through this lesson about modes, have your guitar in hand and play along as we go through each mode so that you can *hear* the differences.

Major Scale Modes

We will continue our mode journey with the seven major modes, which are easily the most popular of the bunch! These modes can be used to add spice to your improvisation, and we can dig deeper to match our modes with specific chords; minor 7, dominant, major 7, and minor 7b5 chords align with our major scale modes. They are incredibly popular in modern music and are ***essential*** tools for professional guitarists.

There are seven major modes in all:

- **Ionian**
- **Dorian**
- **Phrygian**
- **Lydian**
- **Mixolydian**
- **Aeolian**
- **Locrian**

Memorizing all of these shapes can feel a bit daunting, which is why we will switch the order around a bit to make it easier and logical.
Typically, the modes are taught in the order above because that's the natural order. But, to help us get a good understanding of how the modes relate to one another, we will learn the Lydian mode (fourth mode) first, as it allows us to alter one note at a time while we move through the seven modes.

Rather than having to learn new shapes for every mode, all you have to do is take a shape that you are familiar with and lower one of the notes to get your next shape.

The major modes can be placed in order from "brightest" sounding to "darkest" sounding. We will use that idea as our guideline for learning each mode, as detailed below:

- Lydian (Starting Mode)
- Ionian (Lydian + Natural 4)
- Mixolydian (Ionian + b7)
- Dorian (Mixolydian + b3)
- Aeolian (Dorian + b6)
- Phrygian (Aeolian + b2)
- Locrian (Phrygian + b5)

Let's start with the Lydian mode!

Lydian Mode

We begin this part of our mode journey with the Lydian mode, which starts on the fourth scale degree of the major scale. We will be using the note **C** as the root for all of the modes in this lesson to keep things uniform.

The Lydian mode has a whole-half step pattern that looks like this:

Whole-Whole-Whole-Half-Whole-Whole-Half

It is a wonderful mode for those who are looking to craft sounds that are dreamy or absent-minded. It has a very distinct and relaxing sound due to the spacing between the major third and sharp fourth, even though it is fairly close to the major scale in terms of notes. It is often used to convey mystery and dreamy feelings; it is used in the theme from *Back to the Future*, and the theme from *The Simpsons*. The main difference between the major scale and the Lydian mode is that the Lydian mode uses a raised fourth scale degree or **#4.**

Since we are playing C Lydian, and C is the fourth scale degree of the G Major scale, you can almost think of it like playing a G Major scale, though starting with the note C (this is because Lydian is the fourth major mode).

The Lydian mode is built using the following interval pattern:

1-2-3-#4-5-6-7-8
C-D-E-F#-G-A-B-C

Take some time and memorize this formula, as it will act as the starting position for all of the other modes in this lesson.

Once you feel comfortable with the formula and the *idea* of the Lydian mode, here are a few important Lydian fingerings that you can apply to your solos or practice on their own. As always, make sure to use a metronome while you are practicing. Start slow and work your way up, strive for accuracy.
The numbers on the fretboard represent scale degrees; the red numbers on the side show you which fret is at the top.

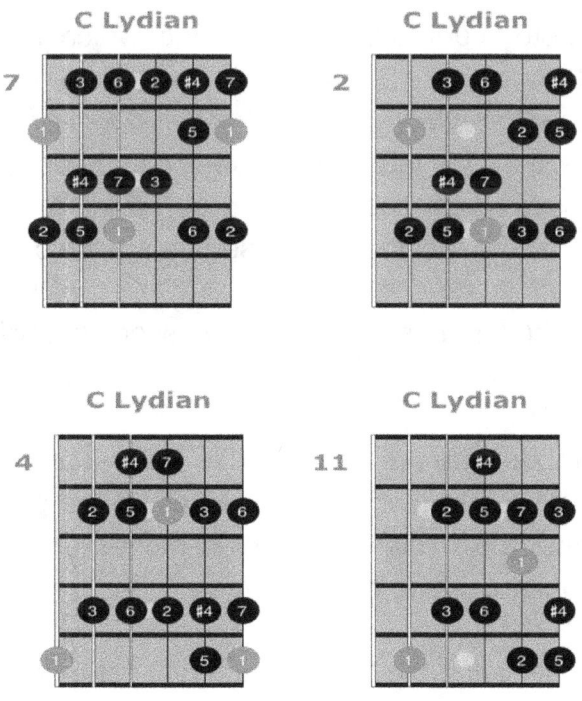

The Lydian Mode in Popular Music

While the Lydian mode is incredibly popular in the world of film music composition, there are plenty of excellent Lydian mode examples in the world of popular music as well.

We highly recommend checking out "Possibly Maybe", which is Bjork's ethereal song off of her album *Post*. The Lydian mode pops up in the intro melody with her vocal.

Joe Satriani's "Flying in a Blue Dream" is a great example of Lydian mode used in a guitar solo. It has a very dreamy and wondrous feeling. The chord structure is based around C Major and Cmaj#11.

"Zoot Allures", which is an old tune by Frank Zappa, has a chord in the beginning that spells out the A Lydian sound. It's a wonderful song to use as a Lydian reference, as it provides you with the sound right off the bat.

Ionian Mode

Now, let's alter one note to get to the Ionian Mode, which is otherwise referred to as the "Major Scale".

Yes, the Ionian mode is simply the major scale. It can be used to solo over Major7 chords, though it has a much softer feel. In our opinion, it is one of the most important modes due to the fact that it is based on the tonic of major chords.

The overall sound of the Ionian scale is usually associated with comfort, positivity or happiness.

To build the Ionian mode, you are going to use the Lydian mode as a reference. Simply lower the fourth of the Lydian by one fret on the guitar. As you'll see in these chord diagrams, the Lydian and Ionian modes are *very* closely related, though they have a unique sound when played.

The Ionian mode is built using the following interval pattern:

1-2-3-4-5-6-7-8
C-D-E-F-G-A-B-C

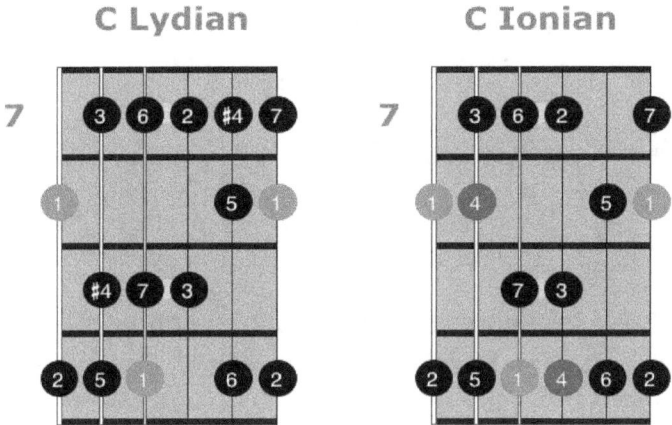

Start by playing the Lydian mode and then move directly to the Ionian mode so that you can see how closely related the two modes are. Once you are ready, you can look at a few different fingers for the Ionian mode on the fretboard.

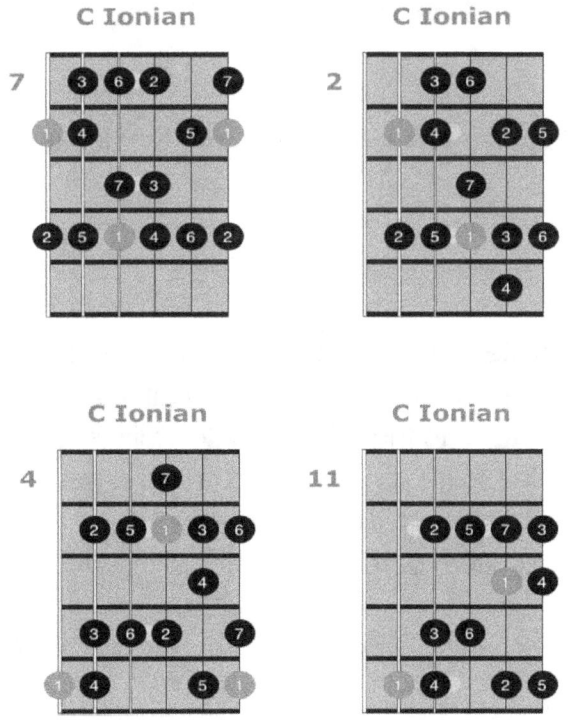

The Ionian Mode in Popular Music

One of the first examples of the Ionian mode that I always seem to think of is Tom Petty's "Free Fallin'", as it is one of the happiest and most uplifting songs around! It is also written in a way that helps people to reminisce, which is another key characteristic of the mode. "Free Fallin'" uses F Ionian.

The chords that are strummed move from F to Fsus4 to F/C. Because the chords in the song center around the F Major chord, the Ionian flavor comes out to emphasize the central F.

Lots of guitar enthusiasts know about Eric Johnson and his hit "Cliffs of Dover". It is another song that exudes positivity. The song is in G. I recommend listening to the lick around 2:20, as it truly establishes the Ionian sound!

Mixolydian Mode

Now that you have the Ionian mode down, let's alter one note from that to get the **Mixolydian mode**, which is the fifth mode of the major scale. The Mixolydian mode can be used in a number of instances, especially when soloing over dominant 7th chords.

The Mixolydian mode has an intervallic structure that looks like this:

1-2-3-4-5-6-b7-8
C-D-E-F-G-A-Bb-C

Guitarists often associate the Mixolydian mode with the blues. It is *very* closely related with the dominant chord, which is why guitarists often play it over dominant chords in progressions. Due to the **b7** in the intervallic structure, the mode is often seen as "darker" than the major scale. The **b7** interval has this desire to resolve to the root, though it is further away than a regular major **7**. This is what gives the Mixolydian mode its signature dominant tension.

Playing C Mixolydian is basically like playing an F Major scale, though starting on the note **C**.

As you'll see in the fretboard diagrams, Ionian and Mixolydian are very closely related. The main difference is the **b7**.

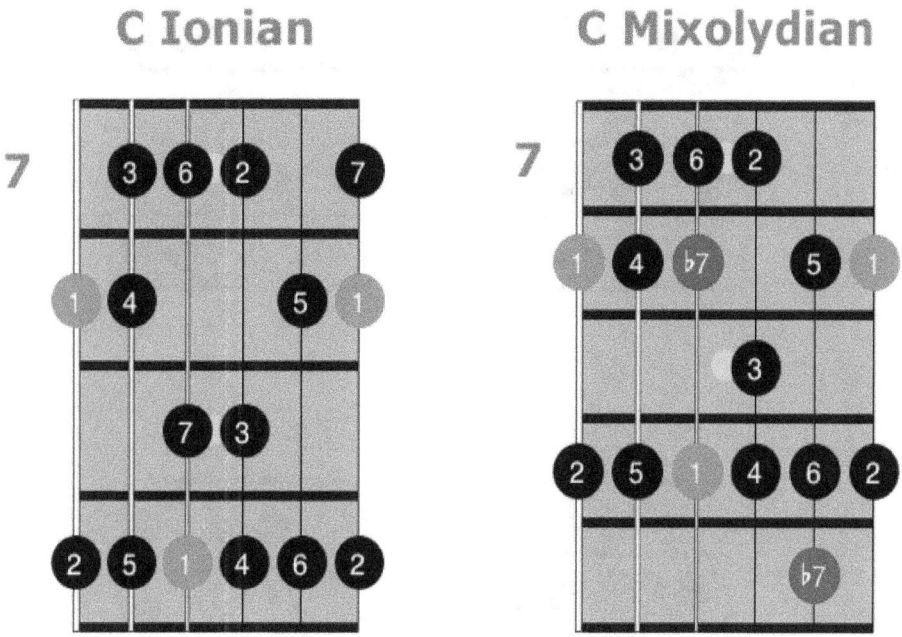

Begin by playing the C Ionian mode before moving directly to the C Mixolydian mode so that you can see how closely they are related.

Once you are ready, you can move on to the four Mixolydian mode fingerings across the fretboard.

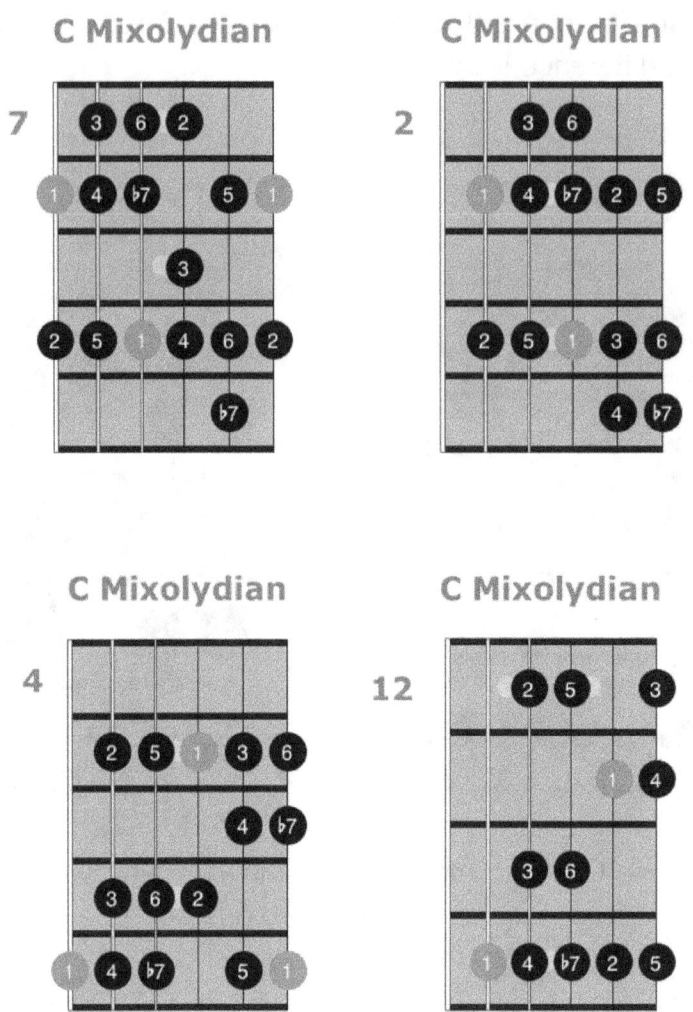

One of the first examples that I always think of when teaching the Mixolydian mode is the song "Walk This Way" by Aerosmith. The famous riff that is used throughout the song uses Mixolydian extensively. "Walk This Way" goes back to the roots of blues by sticking to a dominant sound throughout.

Another classic Mixolydian song comes from the band War. I'm talking about the song "Lowrider". There is no doubt that you've heard this song before, whether on the radio, in films, or on the George Lopez sitcom intro theme that always seemed to be playing somewhere in the house at 3AM (is it just me?). The bassline throughout the song makes use of the G Mixolydian scale, as does the melody.

Dorian Mode

Now that we have gone through all of the major-based modes, let's move on to the minor-based modes. The first in that series is the Dorian mode.

The Dorian mode is great for soloing over minor seven chords and utilizes a unique natural sixth that gives it a distinct flavor compared to other minor modes, which use flat sixths. The Dorian mode is often associated with a minor sound that is smooth. Jazz guitarists will often use the Dorian mode to outline brighter minor scales, and funk guitar players will often use that major sixth in their chords for that classic James Brown type sound.

The intervallic structure of the Dorian mode looks like this:

1-2-b3-4-5-6-b7-8
C-D-Eb-F-G-A-Bb-C

Having a **b3** in there lets you know that it is in fact a minor sound, though that major sixth makes it sound a bit lighter compared to the natural minor scale that we discussed earlier. I often like to associate the sound of the Dorian scale with more easy-going tunes. It invokes a sense of imagination that isn't nearly as "sad" as the minor scale.

Though it might seem like a strange concept, you get the Dorian mode by altering a note of the major Mixolydian mode. All you have to do is lower the third of the Mixolydian mode by one fret on your fretboard. You can think of C Dorian as playing the Bb Major scale, though starting on the note C.

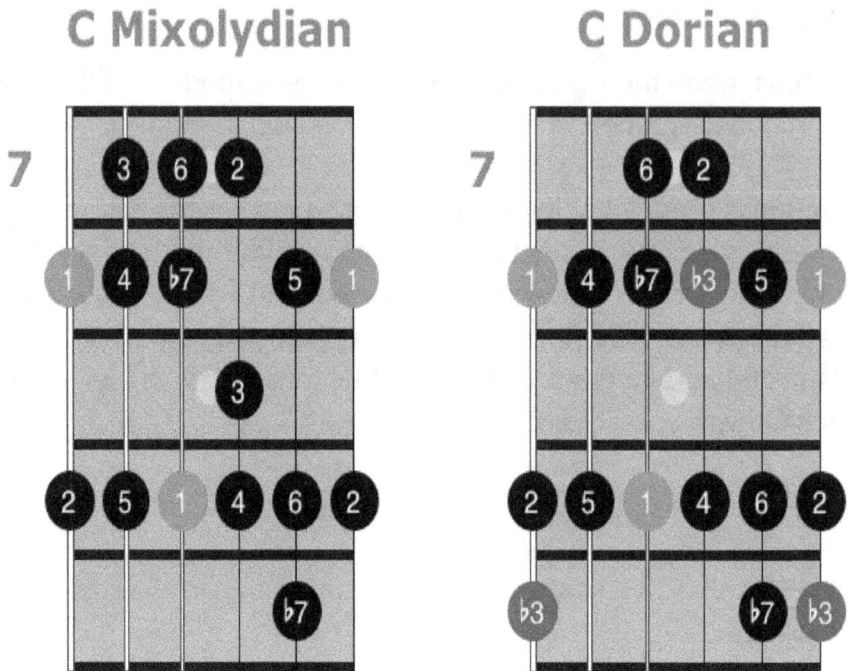

Start by playing the Mixolydian scale and immediately moving to the Dorian mode once you are done to see how closely the two modes match up to one another.

Once you are comfortable with that, you can hop into these four different Dorian fingerings that move up and down the length of the fretboard.

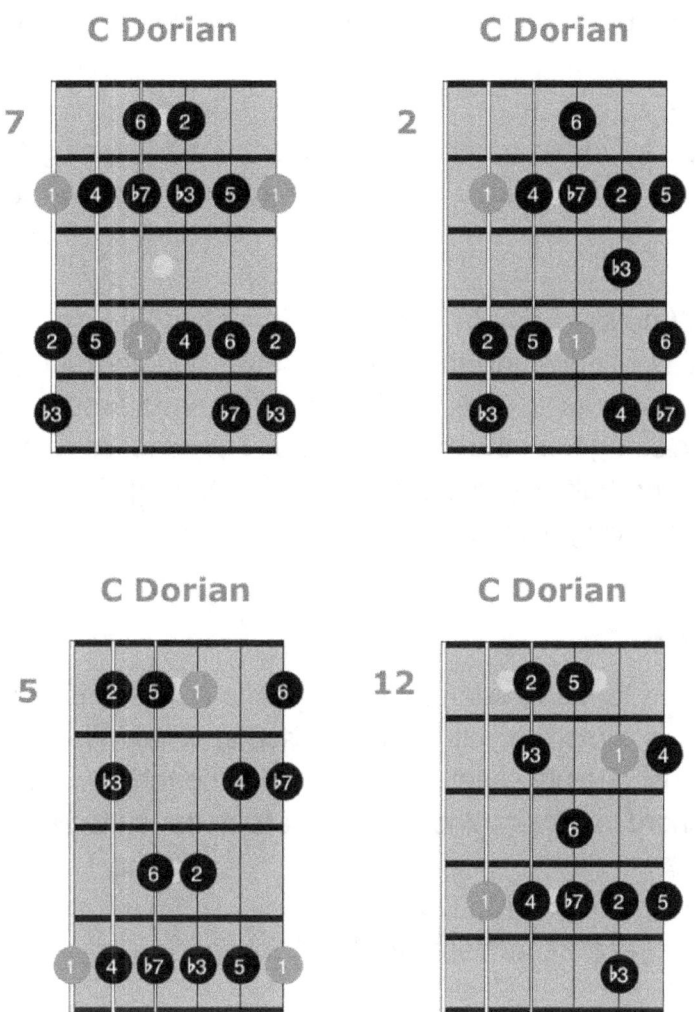

The Dorian Mode in Popular Music

One of the best references for the Dorian mode is Santana. He uses the Dorian mode quite often in his solo. It is also important to note that Latin music in general uses a ton of Dorian music.

"Evil Ways" is a Santana track that uses a chord progression that moves from Gm7 to C7, which outlines G Dorian. As another cool little fact, he does sneak a major sixth into his solo around the 3:26 mark, providing a bit more color for the sound.

If you're studying the Dorian mode, you simply can't do it without looking at Santana.

When studying the Dorian mode, I also recommend listening to David Gilmour, who is the guitarist for Pink Floyd. Gilmour always had such a great ear for outlining modes.

If you listen to "Another Brick In The Wall, Part Two", you will hear that it mostly focuses around D Minor7 and the Dorian mode, bringing out this lighter, cooler minor sound. Make sure to look out for David's bends around 2:20 and 2:40 as well. He bends a string from the root to the major second, creating a Dorian sound, before bending one half-step more to the major third, giving the song a bit more tension before resolving back down.

Aeolian Mode

Now let's move on to the Aeolian mode, which is the sixth in the system of major scale modes. It is simply a natural minor scale, which we investigated earlier. Aeolian is often used to play over minor7 chords, though is *most often* used to play over a minor i chord in a key; minor ii chords are better suited for the Dorian mode.

Jazz players will often resort to Dorian when playing over minor chords, as it has a far more unique jazz sound compared to Aeolian. Aeolian is more popular in the rock sphere.

However, there are a few reasons why the Aeolian mode is extremely important. You can easily change the perspective of chord progressions to surround the sixth chord of the major scale, allowing it to act as the first chord. Essentially, the Aeolian mode provides us with the necessary information to "read" minor chord progressions.

The Aeolian mode is also one of the saddest sounding modes. It is often used by composers to express depth of emotion, like the feeling of yearning, depression, and to bring out that hollow feeling in your chest.

The Aeolian mode looks something like this:

1-2-b3-4-5-b6-b7-8
C-D-Eb-F-G-Ab-Bb-C

You can look at the Aeolian mode compared to the previous mode, which was the Dorian mode. The Aeolian mode is built by simply lowering the sixth of the Dorian mode by a half-step on the guitar. You can see the formula below:

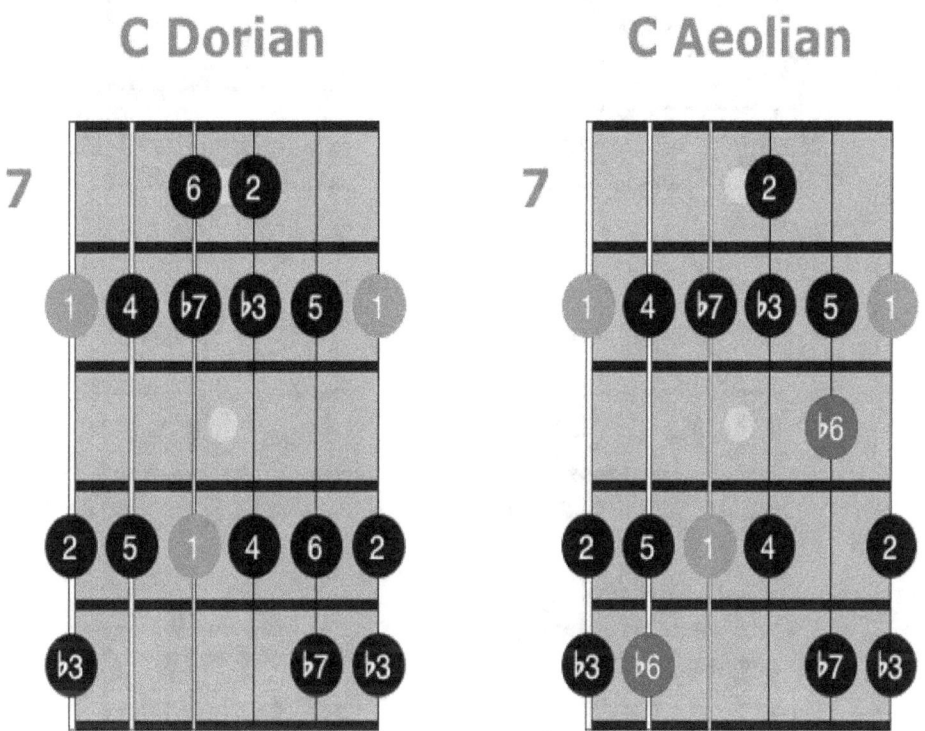

In the next set of diagrams you will see four common fingerings used for the Aeolian mode. Start by getting the first shape down before moving on to the next. Like the other modes, make sure to practice using a metronome and slowly increase the tempo as you get more comfortable. See if you can come out with some melodies of your own while playing these scales.

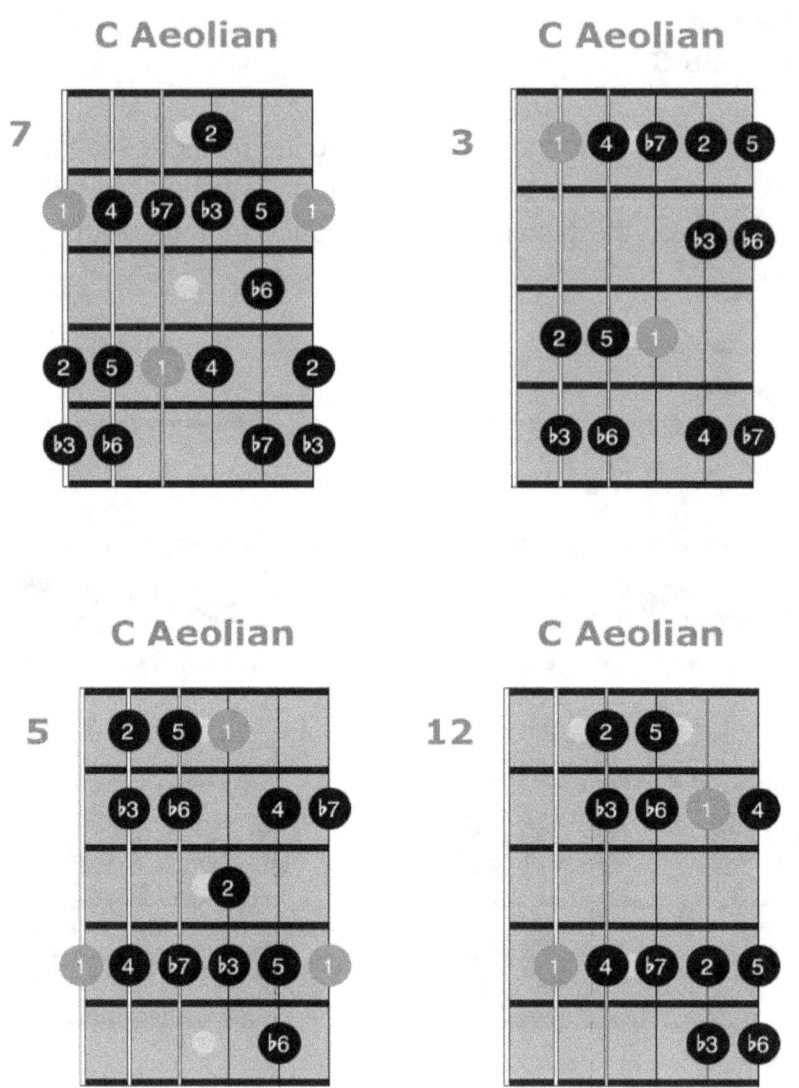

The Aeolian Mode in Popular Music

An excellent example of the Aeolian mode in popular music is the song "Losing My Religion" by REM. The song makes use of A Aeolian as it moves through the verses. The tonal center of the song is the A minor chord. The chord progression for "Losing My Religion" starts with A minor and moves back and forth between that and the fifth chord, which is E minor. It eventually winds up moving to D minor, which is the fourth chord, before completely transitioning out of the minor feel with G in the chorus.

The verses in this song are an excellent representation of Aeolian with their remorseful nature.

Phrygian Mode

Now let's move on to the Phrygian mode, which is the third mode in the major scale. It is also one of the most interesting sounding modes around. Phrygian is very commonly played over minor 7 chords. If you're looking to bring the sounds of Flamenco to your solos, this is definitely the mode to use. Of course, there are many jazz players who use the Phrygian mode too, though it is a bit less common. Phrygian also works nicely over dominant 7th chords if you want to add a bit of flavor. This mode is also often used in heavy metal music as well.

The Phrygian mode looks something like this:

1-b2-b3-4-5-b6-b7-8
C-Db-Eb-F-G-Ab-Bb-C

When you play the Phrygian mode over dominant 7th chords, you can produce b9, #9, and b13 intervals. The Phrygian mode has this wide open sound that packs quite a powerful punch.

Compared to the Aeolian mode, the Phrygian mode is a bit more dissonant sounding due to the fact that the 2 is flat. Of course, it still isn't as "dissonant" as Locrian, though we'll get there! If you're looking to add a sense of mystery or urgency to your songs, the Phrygian mode is an excellent choice.

The Phrygian mode is often used by composers when they want to move a piece in a different direction. It is also used to highlight intriguing moments.

Below is the Phrygian mode, which is built by taking the Aeolian mode and lowering the second by one half-step.

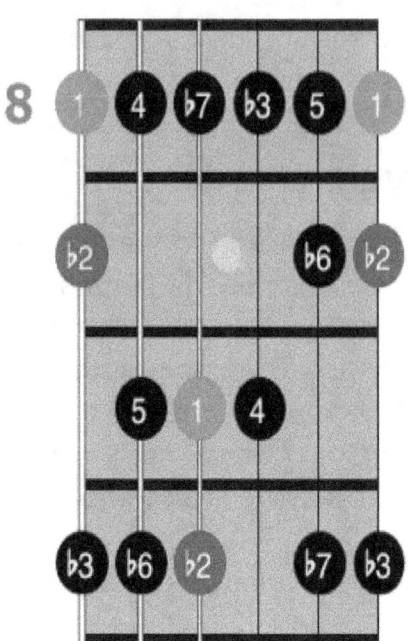

The next set of diagrams includes four fingerings that you can use for the Phrygian mode. Make sure to practice these with a metronome and only increase the speed once you are feeling comfortable.

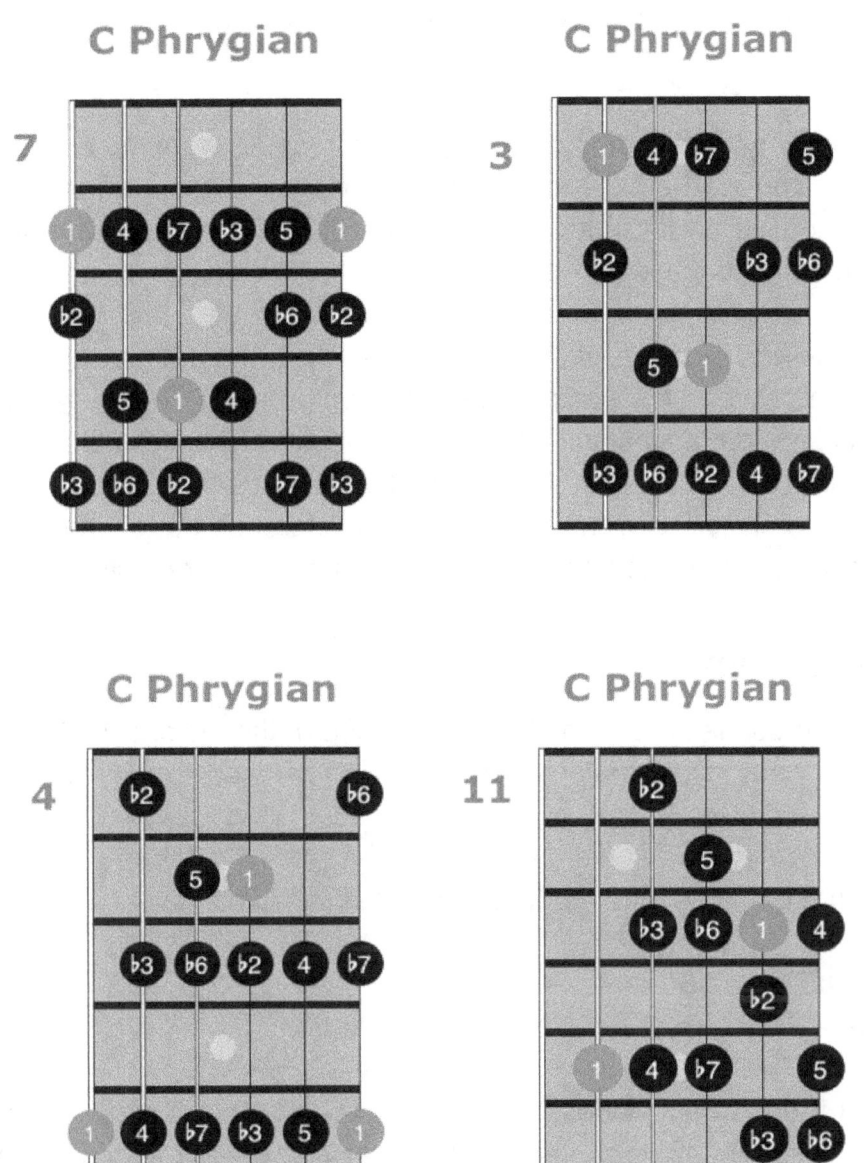

The Phrygian Mode in Popular Music

One of the best points of reference for the Phrygian mode for guitarists is the song "Symphony Of Destruction" by Megadeth. It creates a sense of urgency that only the Phrygian mode can. Plus, even if you're still a beginner guitar player, the riff is fairly easy to play, meaning you can use it as a tool to remember the Phrygian mode!

We hear the Phrygian mode in this song when it moves from the F power chord to the E power chord. The half-step movement between the F power chord and the E power chord is pretty much the central focus of the song. It outlines the E Phrygian mode altogether.

Another excellent example of the Phrygian mode is the Jefferson Airplane song, "White Rabbit". When the bass riff shifts the entire song up one semitone to the flat second, you get an instant Phrygian feel. It provides listeners with a sense of urgency and a tonal shift, exactly like we talked about earlier. Plus, "White Rabbit" is an absolute classic, making it an excellent reference as to what the Phrygian mode has the capability to do within the context of popular music.

Locrian Mode

The Locrian mode is the seventh and final mode of the major scale! It is built from the seventh note in the major scale and is often used to play over minor 7b5 chords.

The structure of the Locrian mode looks something like this:

1-b2-b3-4-b5-b6-b7-8
C-Db-Eb-F-Gb-Ab-Bb-C

Compared to the other modes, the Locrian mode is the darkest, most unstable, and most dissonant mode of the bunch. It has a very dark sound due to the fact that it has minor and diminished intervals. In fact, there is only one perfect interval, the 4th. The dissonance comes into play because of the flattened 2nd and flattened 5th and their relationship to the root. If you want to make something sound like it's about to tip over the edge, the Locrian mode is an excellent choice.

The Locrian mode is even more urgent sounding than the Phrygian mode, as it goes beyond the flattened 2nd. Essentially, it is the Phrygian mode on steroids with the added flattened fifth, giving it a sinister sound overall. This is a great choice for building musical tension.

Because the Locrian mode is so dissonant, it is not the most popular choice when it comes to popular music. However, if you listen to a lot of heavy metal music, you can hear Locrian being alluded to often.

We will compare the Locrian mode to the Phrygian mode. We can build the Locrian mode by lowering the fifth of the Phrygian by one half-step on the fretboard. Look at the diagram below and you will see how we took the C Phrygian mode and lowered the fifth by one half-step in both octaves to get to our Locrian mode:

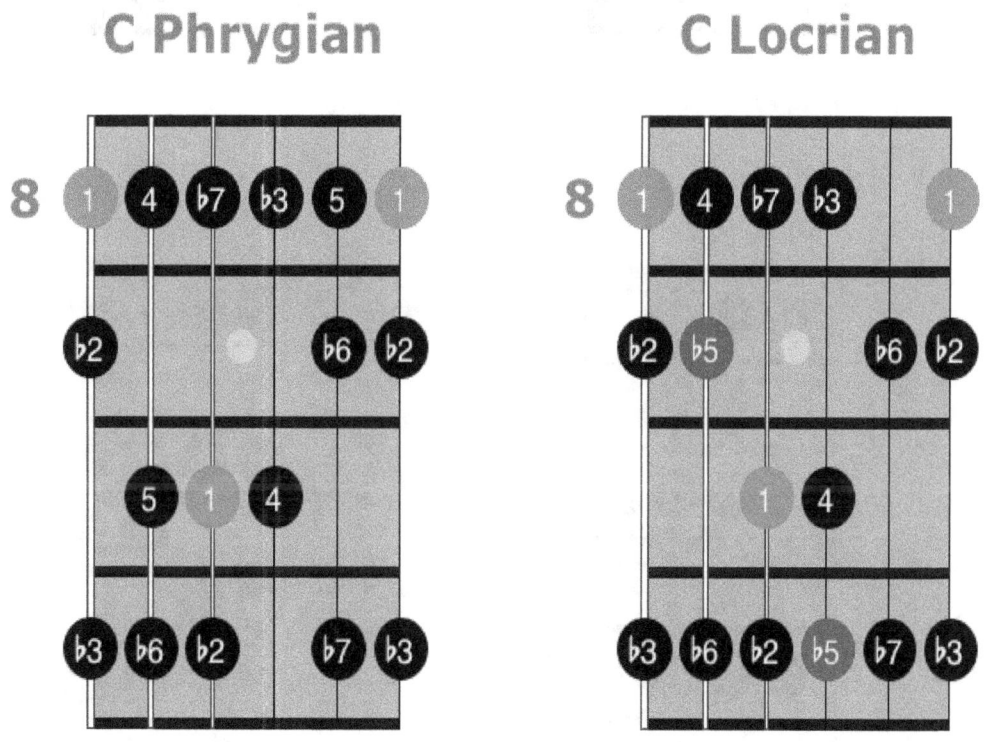

In the next set of diagrams we have the four Locrian fingerings. As always, make sure to use a metronome as you practice these and only speed up once you are feeling comfortable:

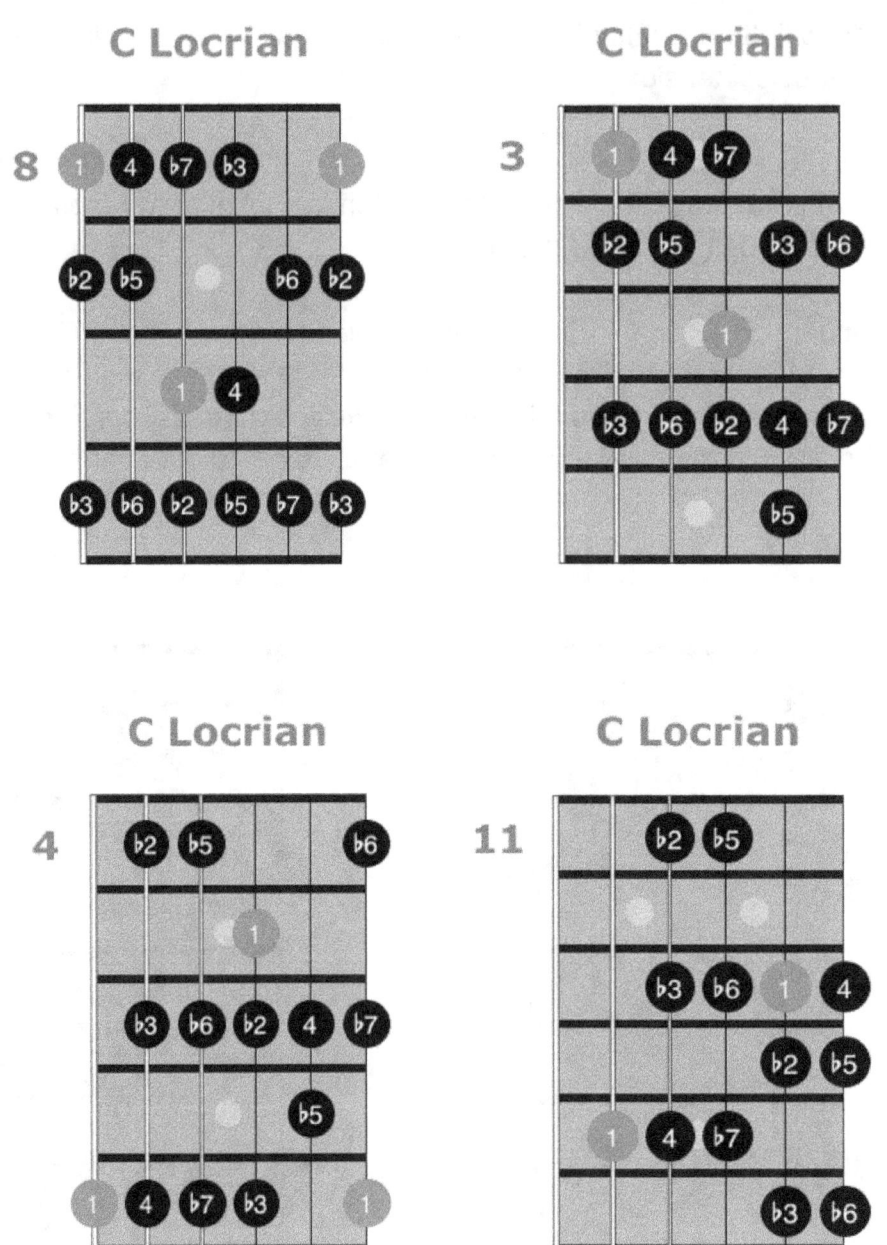

The Locrian Mode in Popular Music

While there aren't many great examples of the Locrian mode in popular music because of its dissonance, we were able to find a few that you can use as references.

Fans of The Strokes will know the song "Juicebox", which is a decent representation of the Locrian mode. The main riff in the song literally moves through the Locrian scale in order, minus the flat 6th, driving the track forward.

Of course, we also mentioned the fact that Locrian is quite often used in heavy metal music to evoke a serious sense of urgency. We can't think of a better band to represent the heavy metal genre than Metallica. The song "Sad But True", makes use of the D Locrian mode, and the song "Blackened" makes use of the E Locrian mode. The riff from "Sad But True" is fairly simple as well, making it an excellent reference point whenever you forget the Locrian mode!

A Summary of the Major Scale Modes

There are many different ways that people go about ordering the modes, and while there are a variety of methods that are useful in their own right, we have found that one of the *best* ways to view the modes is moving from **light** to **dark**. You can almost view the modes as a palette of color.

To do this, you can start by categorizing the modes into Major, Minor, and Half Diminished categories.

The Major modes in this case would include:

Lydian - 1-2-3-#4-5-6-7
Ionian - 1-2-3-4-5-6-7
Mixolydian - 1-2-3-4-5-6-b7

Moving on to the Minor modes, we have:

Dorian - 1-2-b3-4-5-6-b7
Aeolian - 1-2-b3-4-5-b6-b7
Phrygian - 1-b2-b3-4-5-b6-b7

Saving the darkest for last, we have the only half diminished mode:

Locrian - 1-b2-b3-4-b5-b6-b7

One of the reasons that we like to view the modes in this manner is that they will present you with better compositional and improvisational ideas. Thinking about light and dark modes will get you to think about the finer details of each piece of music that you listen to, play, or create. It will help you to hear modes in an effective manner. After all, we don't just practice scales and modes to practice them! We practice them to *use* them in our own playing and writing.

Chapter 9 - Melodic Minor Modes

Melodic minor modes are next, though you might be thinking at this point,

"I just learned SEVEN new shapes, how am I supposed to learn seven more?!"

We feel you, and so that you are not overwhelmed, we want to make this a bit easier for you by tying together your previous knowledge of major modes and these new melodic minor modes. One of the best ways to view the melodic minor modes is by thinking of them as major modes with one note of each of the modes lowered.

This is great reference for those of you looking to really get your hands dirty with bebop improvisation, or if you're interested in learning vocabulary that's more "out of the box".

Let's take a look at the seven melodic minor modes and how they compare with the major modes:

- Jazz Minor (Ionian with b3)
- Dorian b2 (Dorian with b2)
- Lydian Augmented (Phrygian with b1)
- Lydian Dominant (Lydian with b7)
- Mixolydian b6 (Mixolydian with b6)
- Locrian Natural 2 (Aeolian with b5)
- Super Locrian (Locrian with b4)

So that's the gist of melodic minor modes, let's dig a bit deeper into each of the melodic minor modes to see how we can apply it to our playing.

Jazz Minor - Melodic Minor Mode 1

The first one is pretty easy, as the Jazz Minor mode is the same exact thing as the Melodic Minor scale. The reason that many refer to it as the "jazz minor mode" is that it distinguishes it from the regular melodic minor scale that we use, though technically they share the same pattern.

The structure of the Jazz Minor mode is:

1-2-b3-4-5-6-7-8
C-D-Eb-F-G-A-B-C

The jazz minor mode is essentially a major scale with a **b3** and it is often used over minor chords with added major sevenths. This is a *very* common chord in the realm of jazz. It helps to create tension thanks to the raised seventh. Some players find the tension a bit off putting, though many find it to be quite enjoyable. It is a mode that takes some experimentation to get the right feel for.

To get a better idea of the Jazz Minor or Melodic Minor mode, we will compare it to the Ionian mode. Simply lower one note, which is the third in this case, to form Jazz Minor. Even with the one note difference, you will realize how unique the sound of the Jazz Minor mode is.

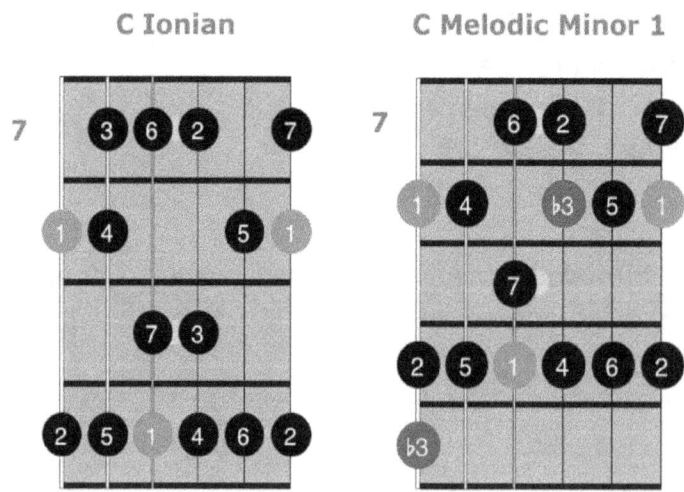

The next set of diagrams will show you how to play the Jazz Minor mode:

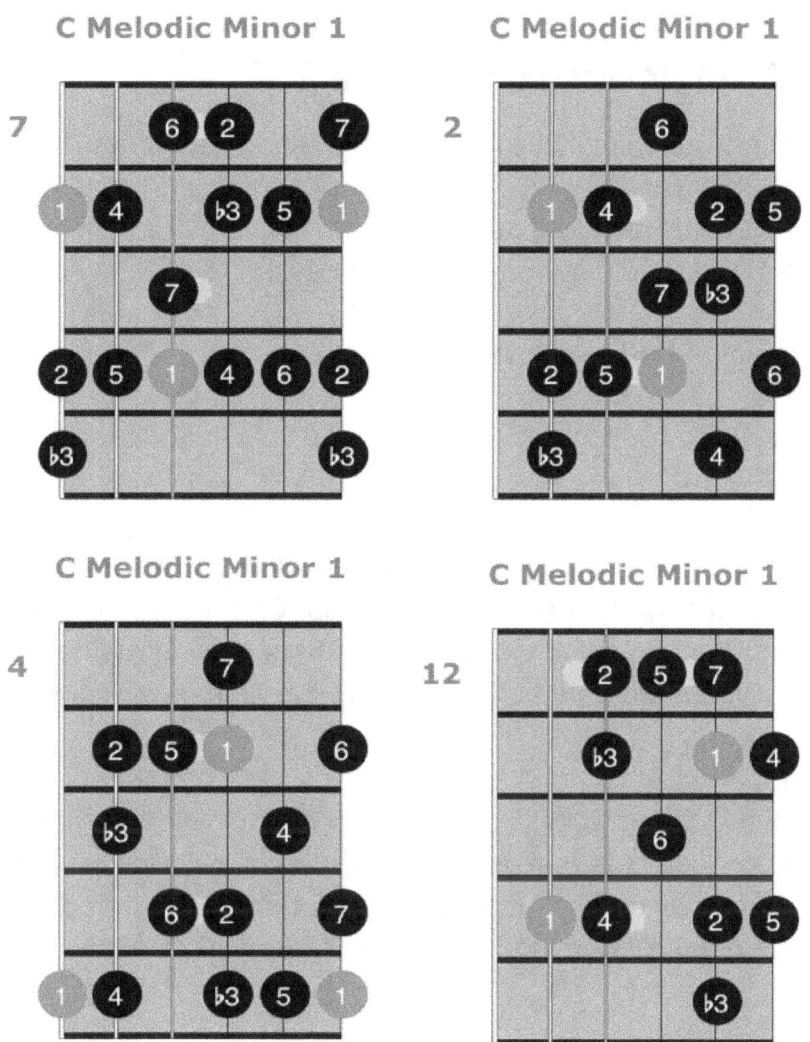

The Jazz Minor Mode in Popular Music

Some great jazz standards that use the minor chord with an added major seventh include "Salt Water" by Julian Lennon or the popular jazz standard, "Nature Boy".

As you will see, this mode is often used between regular minor chords and minor seventh chords. Listen to these songs and try to play your Jazz Minor mode atop them.

Dorian b2 - Melodic Minor Mode 2

The second mode in the melodic minor scale is known as Dorian b2. It can also be referred to as Phrygian #6, though it depends on how you want to look at it. One of the reasons people refer to it as Phrygian #6 is that it would be enharmonic with the Phrygian mode if it did not have the major sixth.

The structure of the Dorian b2 mode is:

1-b2-b3-4-5-6-b7-8
C-D-Eb-F-G-A-Bb-C

The Dorian b2 mode is not a scale that we see often, though it can be really pretty when playing that added b9 on a Dorian vamp. Of course, the issue with adding that b9 is that it has potential to clash with others playing the natural 9, which is very common in Dorian vamps. This is why the Dorian b2 takes some serious planning.

We will use the Dorian mode to build the Dorian b2 melodic minor mode, as the difference of only one note makes it quite easy. Simply lower the 2nd of the major scale Dorian mode by one half-step on the fretboard. Even though Dorian b2 may be pretty close to the Dorian mode, it has a unique characteristic all its own.

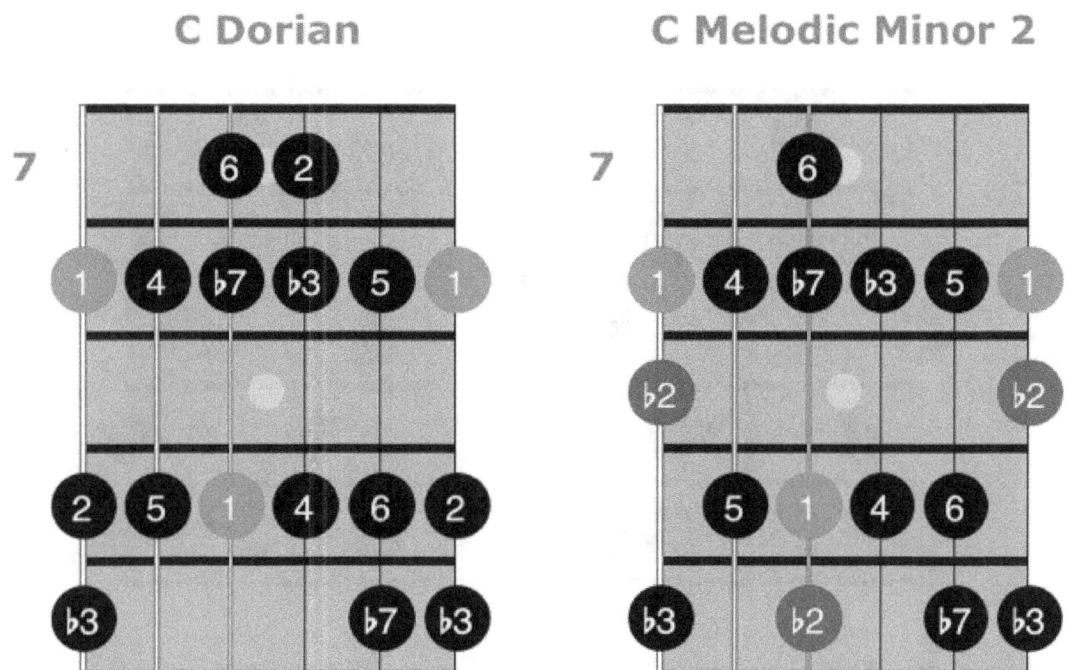

The next set of diagrams shows all of the fingerings that you will use for the Dorian b2 or C Melodic Minor 2:

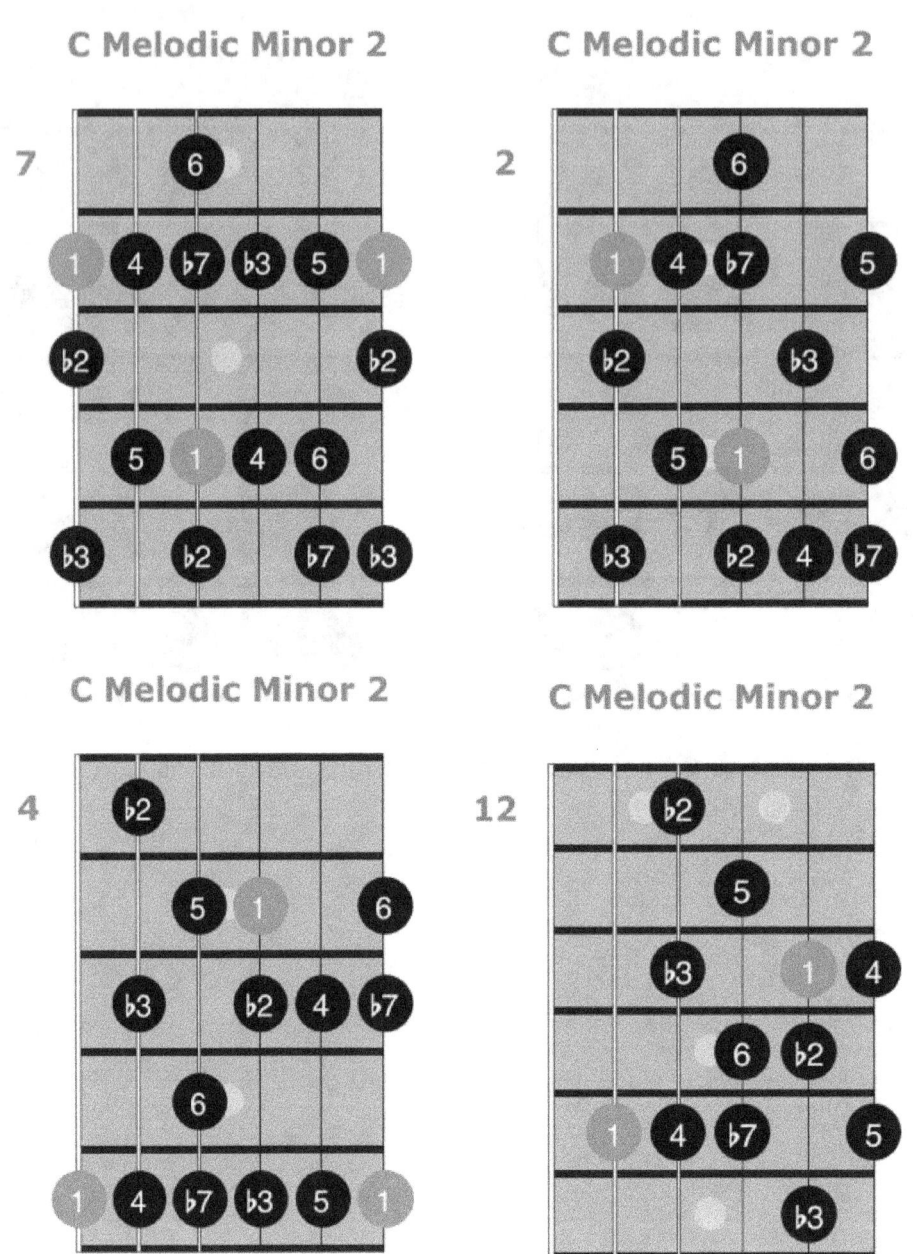

The Dorian b2 Mode in Popular Music

Like we said before, the Dorian b2 is not very common in popular music. However, if you listen to a lot of Assyrian music (that is, Syriac folk music), especially within the genre of folk or dance, you will find the Dorian b2. This is because Assyrian music traditionally makes use of the Phrygian mode. Because the Dorian b2 alters the minor sixth to the major sixth, it adds a bit of lightness while retaining the Assyrian tradition of the Phrygian mode.

Lydian Augmented - Melodic Minor Mode 3

Let's move on to the third mode of Melodic Minor, which is known as the Lydian Augmented mode. The Lydian Augmented Mode is quite unique with a raised fourth and fifth in its scale. Thanks to the fact that it also utilizes the major third and the major seventh, it is the perfect mode for soloing over major seventh chords.

It's definitely not one of the most commonly used modes around, though if you end up playing over a major7#5 chord, or a vamp that uses an extended Lydian mode, you might want to explore the Lydian Augmented. This mode is a good tool for getting that "spacey", dream-sequence type sound.

The structure of the Lydian Augmented mode is:

1-2-3-#4-#5-6-7-8
C-D-E-F#-G#-A-B-C

The Lydian Augmented is built using a lowered root of the Phrygian mode. You can see it in comparison with the Lydian Augmented mode below:

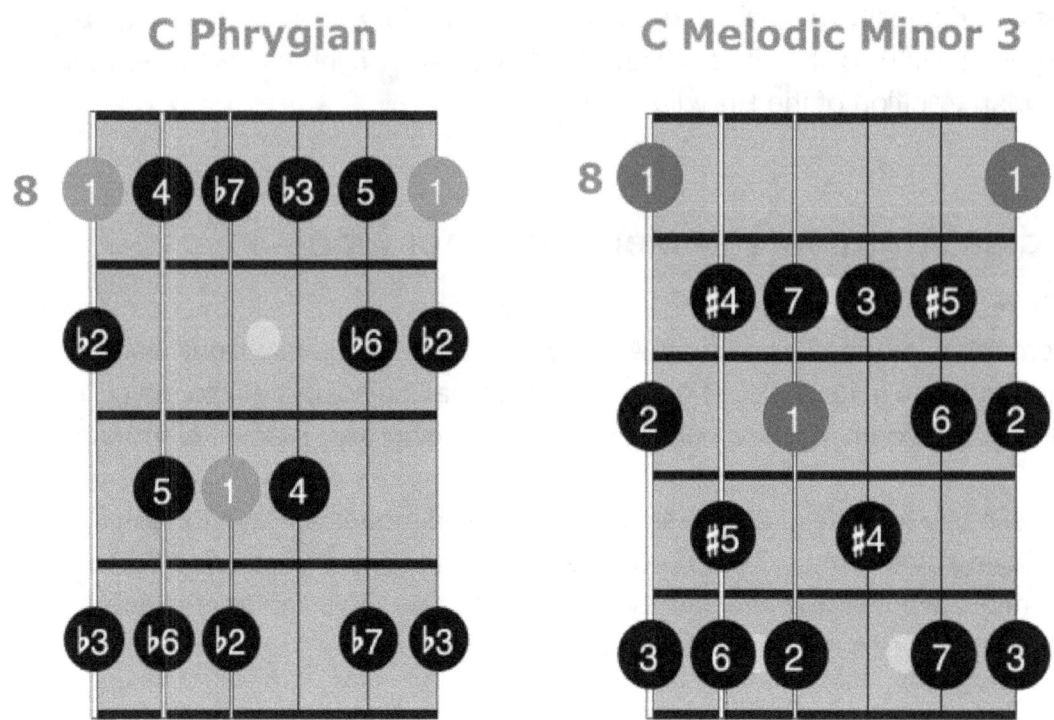

The next set of diagrams shows the four fingerings for the Lydian Augmented mode.

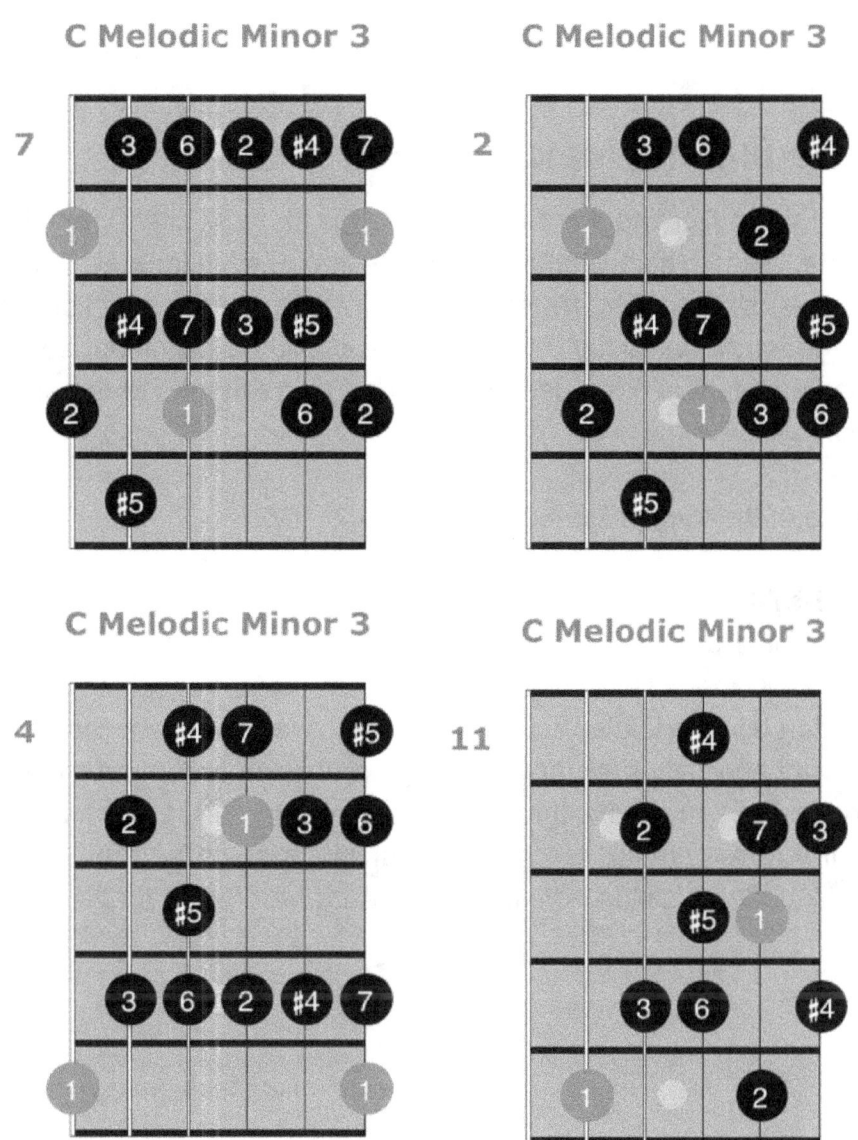

The Lydian Augmented Mode in Popular Music

The Lydian Augmented mode should be thought of more as a choice when certain chords come around, especially the major7#5 chord. It can be heard from a ton of artists such as John Coltrane, Miles Davis, or Woody Shaw. Like many of the other melodic minor modes, Lydian Augmented most naturally finds its place in jazz music.

Lydian Dominant - Melodic Minor Mode 4

Building the Lydian Dominant mode only requires that you alter one note from your Lydian mode. The Lydian Dominant lowers the Lydian mode's seventh scale degree by one half-step. The reason that we refer to it as the Lydian Dominant is that it has the #4 of the Lydian mode and the b7 of the Dominant seventh chord. The Lydian Dominant is often used in jazz and blues thanks to the sweet tension that it adds.

The structure of the Lydian Dominant mode is:

1-2-3-#4-5-6-b7-8
C-D-E-F#-G-A-Bb-C

Guitarists often use the Lydian Dominant to play over Dominant chords, hence the name. This is especially true for 7#11 chords, though it can definitely be played over a regular 7, 9, 11, or 13. It is worth noting that the #11 is enharmonic to the b5, which if you remember, we have in our blues scale as the "blue note". It's essentially like adding a blue note into a standard Mixolydian mode, in place of the 4th.

Look at the Lydian Dominant mode compared to the regular Lydian mode below:

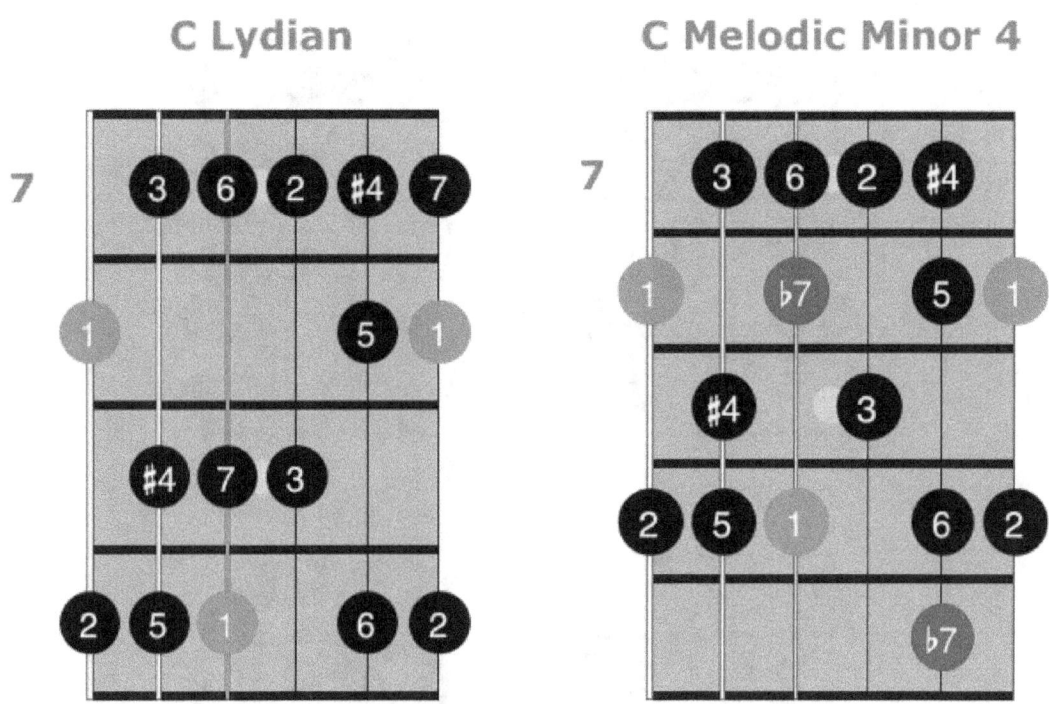

The next set of diagrams shows the four Lydian Dominant fingerings, which you can use for soloing or improvisation:

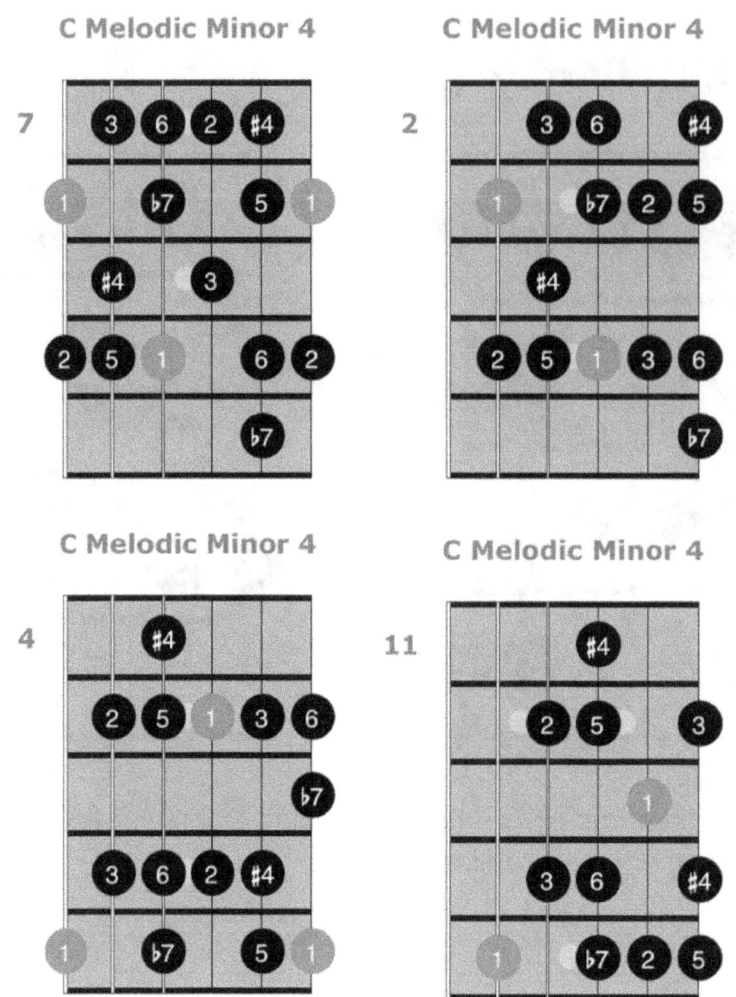

The Lydian Dominant Mode in Popular Music

One of the best examples of the Lydian Dominant mode in popular music is the theme song for *The Simpsons.* As one of the most popular melodic minor modes, it can be found in a variety of different types of music.

Another great example is *Flying In A Blue Dream* by Joe Satriani. A fair amount of Joe Satriani's music utilizes the Lydian Dominant. A more unique example is the song *Pavlov's Daughter* by Regina Spektor, which has some excellent Lydian Dominant a few minutes in.

Mixolydian b6 - Melodic Minor Mode 5

The next mode in the Melodic Minor Mode series is the fifth mode, known as Mixolydian b6. It is built by lowering the sixth scale degree of the Mixolydian mode by one half-step. It has a bit of a sour sound when you play it over dominant chords due to the b6, meaning it needs to be used very carefully.

The structure of the Mixolydian b6 mode is:

1-2-3-4-5-b6-b7-8
C-D-E-F-G-Ab-Bb-C

Look at the two diagrams below to see how Mixolydian b6 compares to the standard Mixolydian mode.

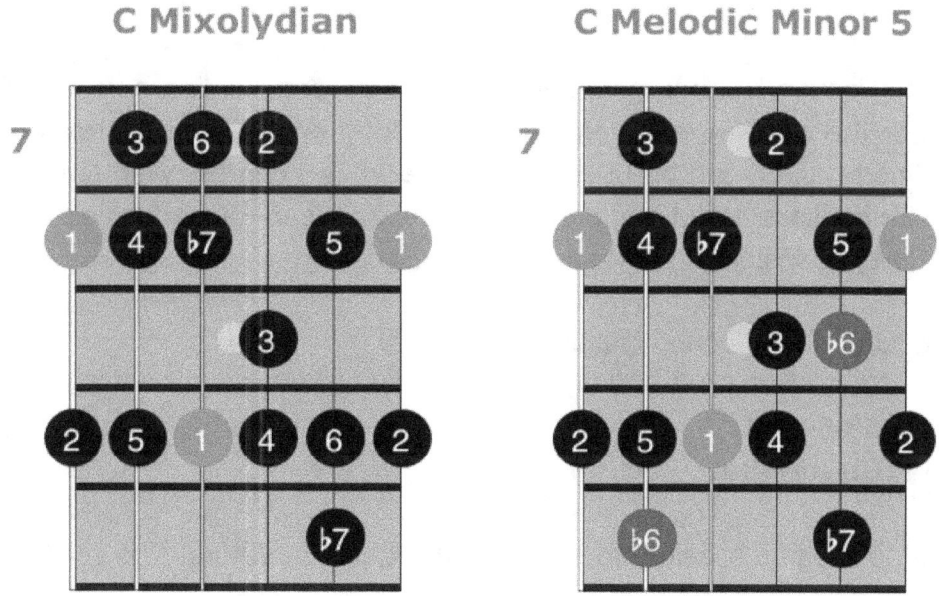

The Mixolydian b6 Mode in Popular Music

It's almost impossible to find the Mixolydian b6 in popular music due to the fact that it doesn't sound that great to Western ears. With that said, it is sometimes referred to as the "Hindu Scale" thanks to its use in Indian music. It is known as Mela Carukesi, Raga Tarangini, or Raga Charukeshi.

Mixolydian b6 is often used in regular major keys when borrowing the bVII dominant 7 chord. One of the most popular bVII dominant 7 chords is "Christmas Is Here", which is *in* F Major, though cycles between F Major7 and EbMaj9#11.

Locrian Natural 2 - Melodic Minor Mode 6

The sixth melodic minor mode in the series is Locrian Natural 2. It is often used to solo over minor 7b5 chords. Many people like to consider it a Locrian mode, as it *can* be used as an alternative in a few different ways. However, it is a bit difficult to use this mode without having it sound like it was an accident. This is due to the fact that the Natural 2 or Natural 9 can be a bit tough to figure out sound-wise, since it tends to sound best used only over the ii chord in a minor ii-V-i chord progression.

To get the Locrian Natural mode, you simply alter one Aeolian note, specifically, the fifth of the Aeolian is lowered. The fingering is very closely related to the Aeolian mode and it can be used to solo over m7b5 chords. With that said, you need to be cautious about using the natural 9, as it can cause tension due to the fact that it is the Major 3 in a regular ii-V-I progression.

The structure of the Locrian Natural 2 mode is:

1-2-b3-4-b5-b6-b7-8
C-D-Eb-F-Gb-Ab-Bb-C

Look at the diagrams below to see how the Locrian Natural 2 is related to the Aeolian:

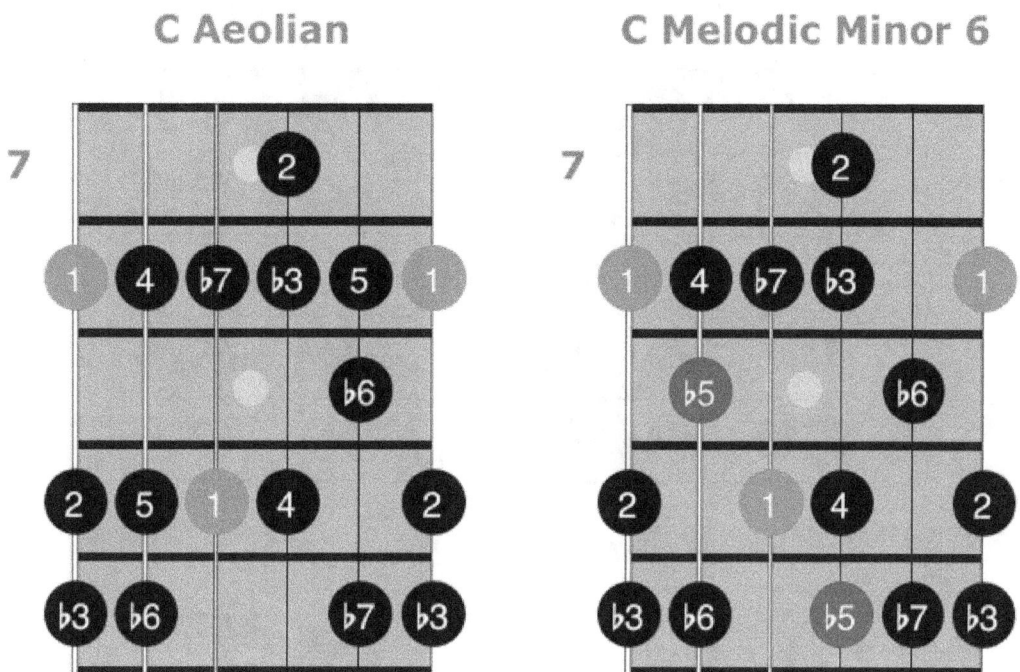

The next four sets of diagrams will give you a better idea of how you can use the Locrian Natural 2 up and down the length of the fretboard.

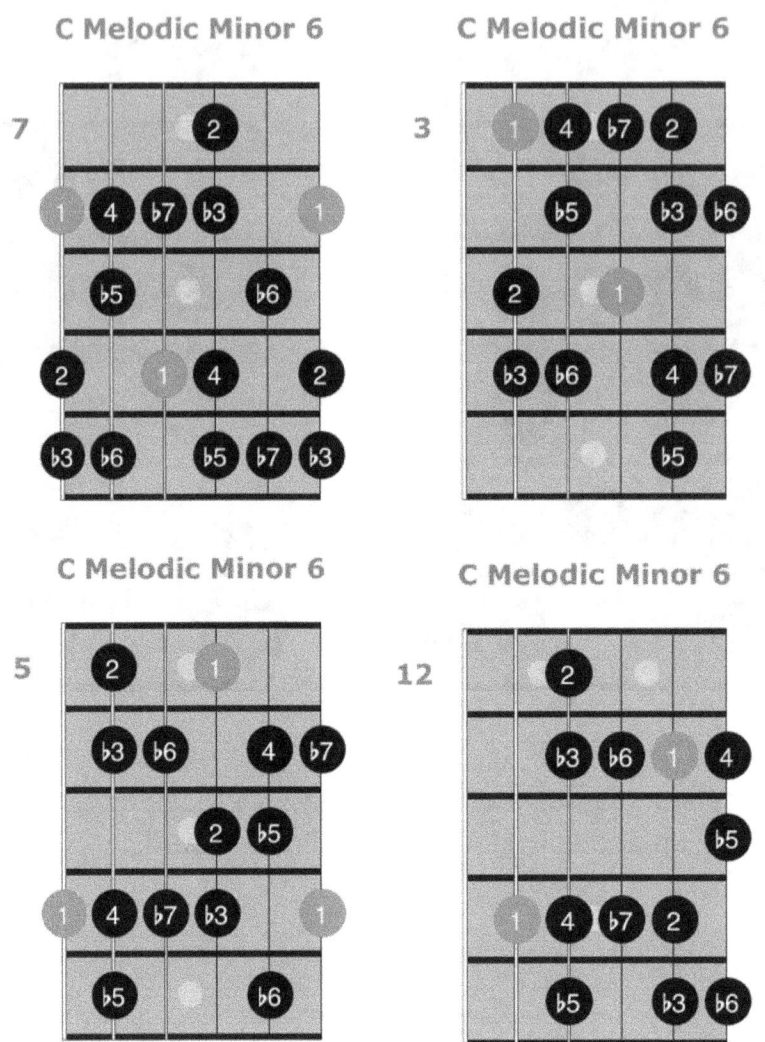

Locrian Natural 2 in Popular Music

Locrian Natural 2 is often played over Locrian mode progressions in jazz. As we said before, it is often played over m7b5 chords in jazz progressions. The color of the Locrian Natural 2 mode is very reminiscent of guitarists like Pat Metheny. We would highly recommend listening to some Pat tunes to get a good idea of the Locrian Natural 2.

Super Locrian - Melodic Minor Mode 7

Ah yes.

We have finally arrived at the end of the Melodic Minor Mode series with the Super Locrian. It is sometimes referred to as the "altered scale" and is very popular on a wide variety of instruments beyond the guitar. It is perfect for creating a bit of tension over dominant chords. The Super Locrian is often used atop major and minor ii-V-I chord progressions in jazz and blues.
With that said, it does take a bit of practice to get used to utilizing the tension found within this mode.

The structure of the Super Locrian mode is:

1-2-b3-4-5-6-7-8
C-Db-Eb-*Fb-Gb-Ab-Bb-C
Fb is the enharmonic equivalent of an E natural; we can only have one of each note in a scale or mode and we already have an Eb.

The best way to think of Super Locrian is by thinking of it compared to standard Locrian. This is because the Super Locrian is built by lowering the fourth scale degree of the Locrian scale. Even though it is closely related to the Locrian mode, it is perfect for use atop dominant seventh chords, especially when you want to stretch the intervals into the b9, #9, b5, and #5 atmospheres.

Look at the two diagrams below to get a better idea of the Super Locrian mode:

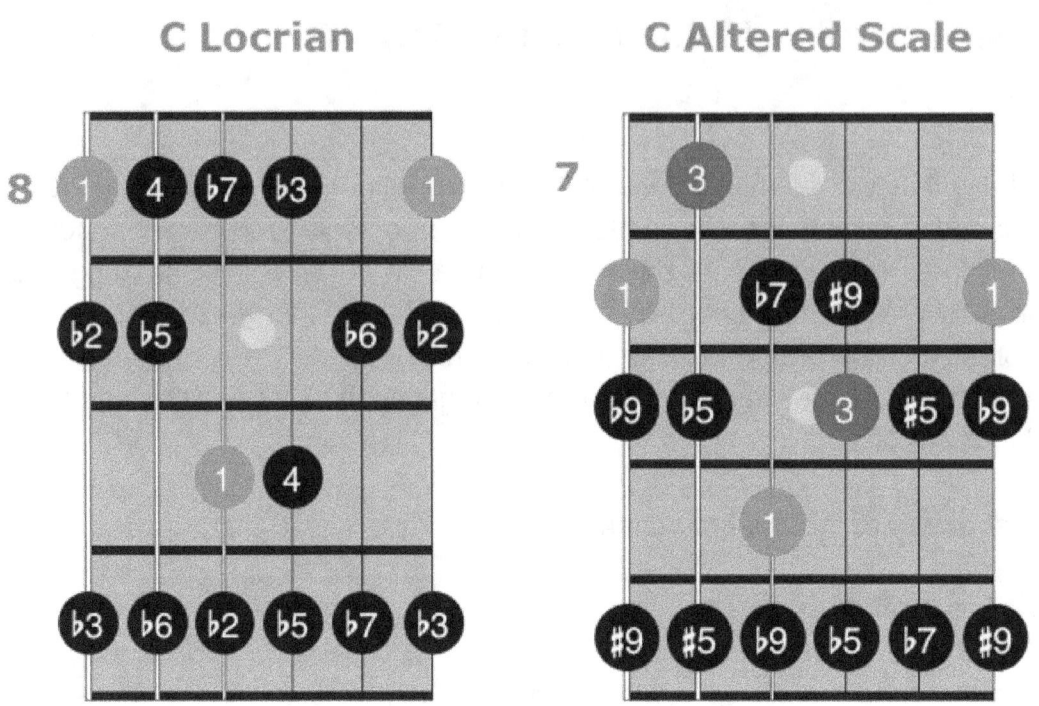

The next set of Super Locrian diagrams will teach you how to play the mode using different fingerings:

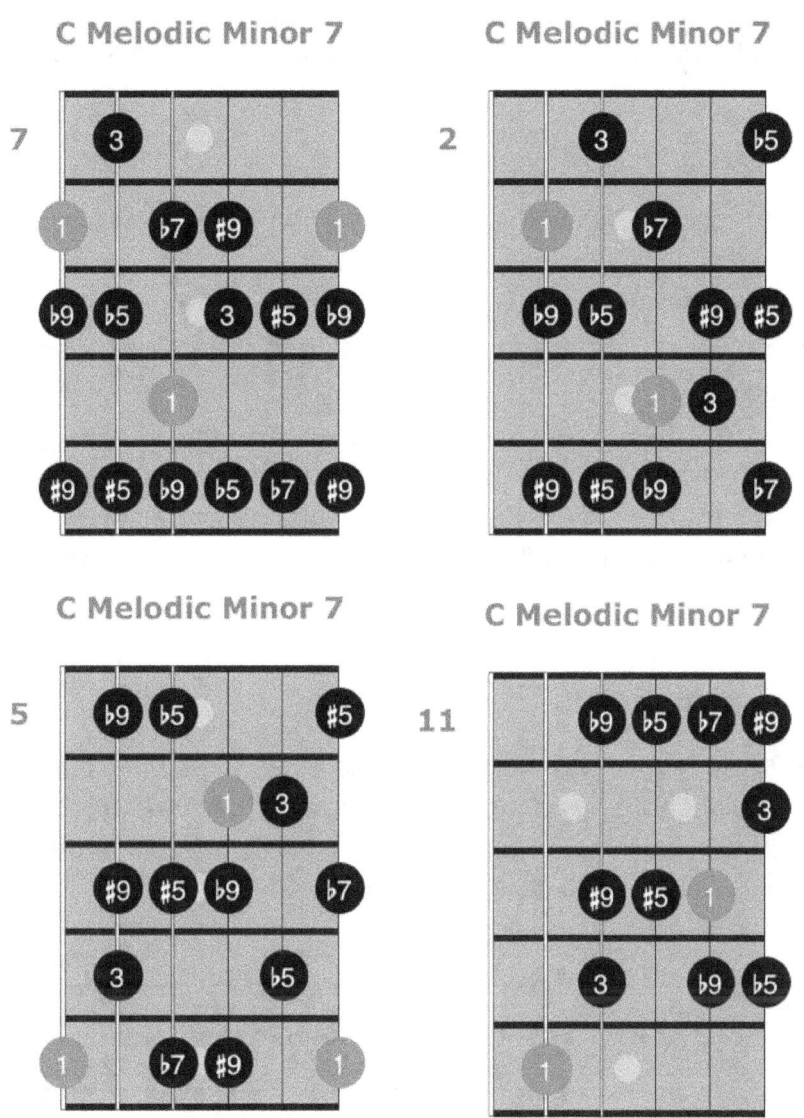

Super Locrian in Popular Music

Super Locrian is typically played over 7alt chords, which are seen a lot in jazz. You can also play it over a rock or fusion tune when a dominant chord comes along. We would recommend listening to Charlie Parker, John Scofield, Mike Stern, Scott Henderson, and Alan Holdsworth. They utilize the super Locrian in a number of different songs when alt7 chords come around in the progressions.

Chapter 10 - Exotic Scales

The scales and modes that we have discussed so far can keep any guitarist busy for a long time. Practicing them deliberately, learning what sounds you enjoy when composing or improvising, and wrapping your ears around these new sounds will take some time. For your reference we are going to continue with some of the most common exotic scales.

In this chapter, we are going to look at a few scales from around the world. To keep things uniform, we will be starting each of these scales on A, though you can move these scales around to different root notes just like every other scale or mode in this book.

Arabian Guitar Scale

The Arabian scale is quite a unique scale, as it has eight different notes; we refer to a scale with eight notes as an "octatonic" scale. The Arabian scale, specifically, is an octatonic *minor* scale; in fact, it is the same as the whole-half version of the diminished scale, which we will get into in a bit.

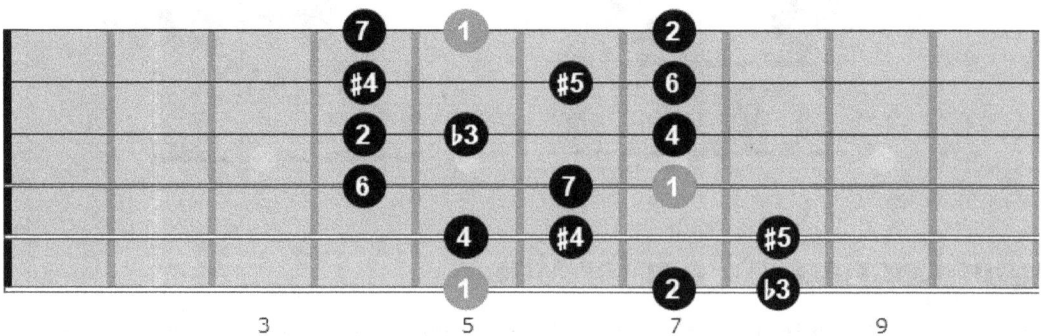

Persian Guitar Scale

The Persian Guitar Scale can be thought of as a major scale that uses a **b2, b5,** and **b6.**

The scale is characterized by its liberal half-step use, as it has four half-steps in total. It also has two instances of augmented seconds and it uses chromaticism quite frequently. Another way to see this scale is as the Locrian mode with major third and seventh degrees.

It looks something like this:

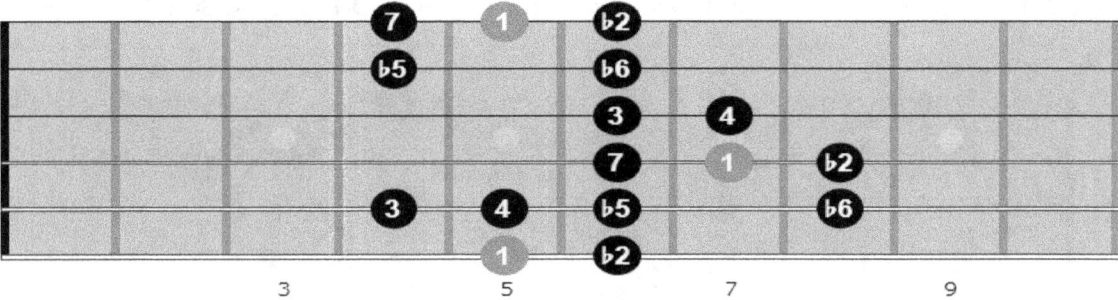

Byzantine Guitar Scale

The Byzantine guitar scale can be thought of as a major scale with a **b2** and **b6**. Some people refer to the scale as the double harmonic scale, the Bhairav Raga, the Mayamalavagowla, or the Maqam Hijaz Scale. The unique gaps in this scale may sound very unfamiliar to western ears.

The reason that it is referred to as the double harmonic scale is because it utilizes two harmonic tetrads that feature augmented seconds. A great example of the Byzantien scale is *Misirlou* by Nikolas Roubanis.

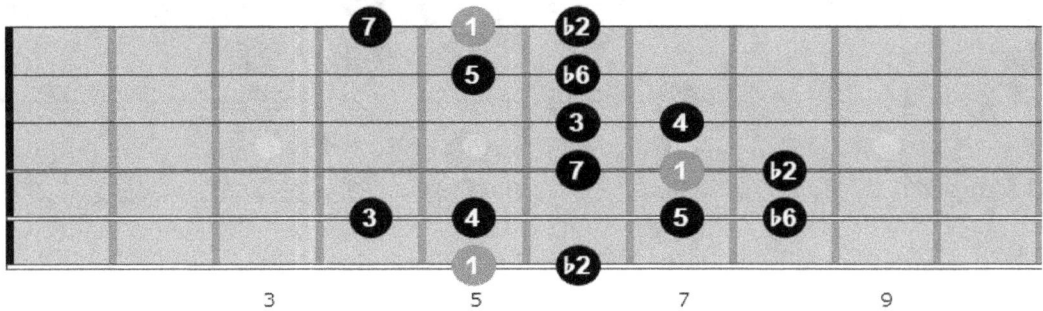

Egyptian Guitar Scale

Egyptian music uses a variety of different scales; a popular one in Egyptian music is the Dorian mode. However, here we have an Egyptian Pentatonic scale. You can think of this scale as the minor pentatonic with a major 2nd instead of a minor 3rd.

It is built on five notes, which is why we refer to it as a pentatonic scale.

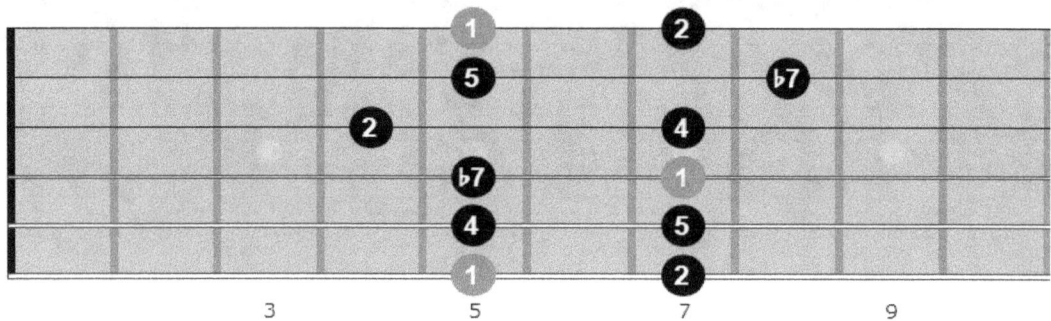

Oriental Guitar Scale

The Oriental Guitar Scale uses seven notes, like most of our conventional scales and modes. We can think of it as a dominant scale—that is, a scale that outlines the major 3rd and flat 7th of a dominant 7th chord— which contains a **b2** and a **b5**. This particular scale is Chinese in origin, though it should not be confused with the Chinese scale. The scale is characterized by groups of semi-note intervals.

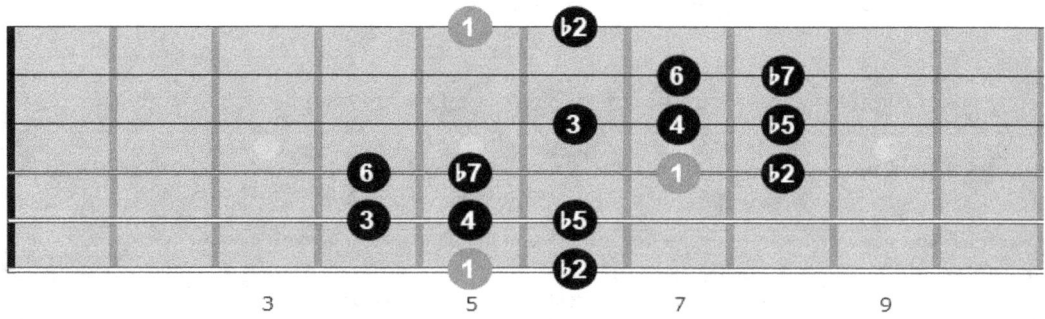

Japanese Guitar Scale

The Japanese scale is a pentatonic scale, though it is unique because it does not contain a third and it uses a b6. Because there is not a third, it is neither major nor minor.

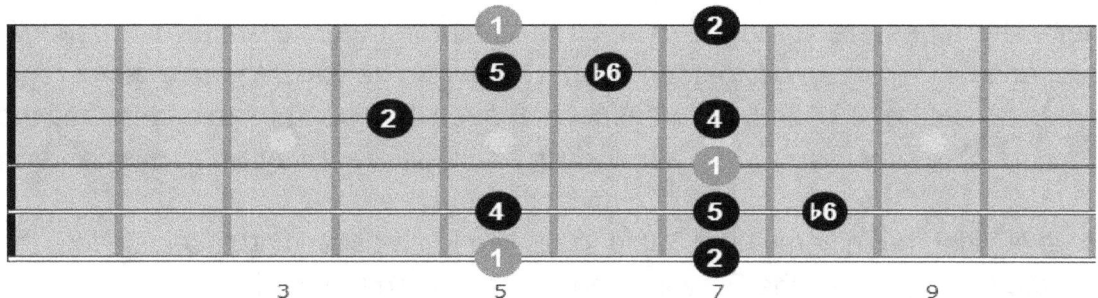

For a fuller version of the Japanese guitar scale, I highly recommend looking at the Hirajoshi scale. The Hirajoshi scale was originally used in shamisen music. A shamisen, for those of you who don't know, is a three-stringed traditional Japanese instrument.

Today, this minor scale is used in jazz and rock music.

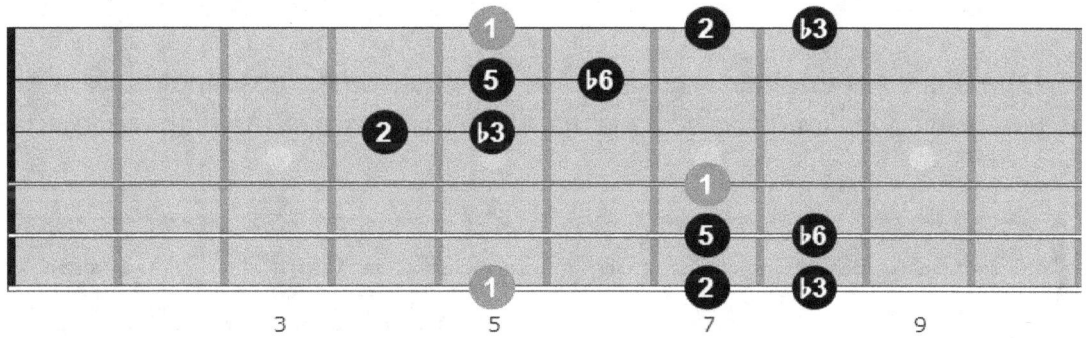

Indian Guitar Scale

The Indian scale has risen to prominence in popular western music. Just think back to old tunes by The Beatles. This particular Indian scale is called the Asavari scale. It is otherwise referred to as raga Asavari.

On a side note, **ragas** are important to understand for those looking to get into Indian music. You can think of a raga as a mix between a composition and a scale.

Raga are musical frameworks that use different tones. They are often used to play or improvise in specific compositions, just like chords and scales are used by jazz musicians to improvise in different jazz pieces.

It is *also* important to note that ragas utilize very specific melodic movements as well. The tones are arranged in a bit of a hierarchy. Each tone uses specific intonation, duration, and ornamentation. Of course, getting into the topic of ragas would constitute an entirely different book, though it is important to understand that they are played one way when **ascending** and a *different* way when **descending.**

Here is what the Indian Guitar Scale looks like in an ascending fashion. Note that it is the same thing as the Phrygian mode without the **b3** and **b7**:

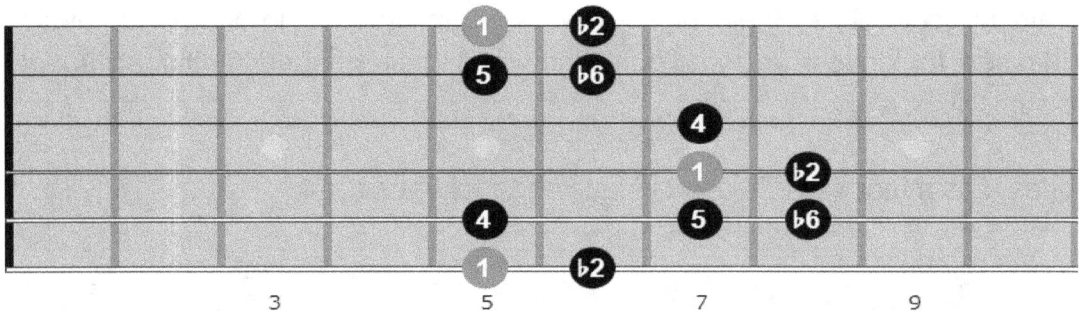

Now, here is what the Indian guitar scale looks like when descending. Note that the descending Indian guitar scale is the same thing as the Phrygian mode:

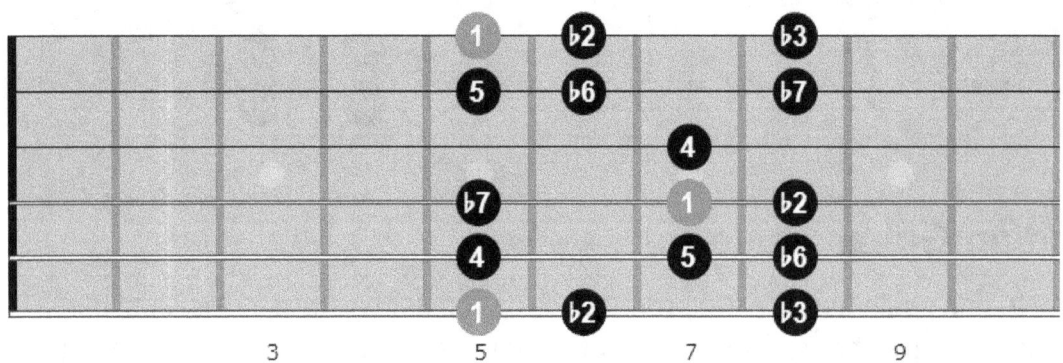

Hungarian Gypsy Minor Guitar Scale

The Hungarian Gypsy Minor guitar scale can be seen as a harmonic minor scale with a **#4**. Bireli Lagrene and Stochello Rosenberg are two guitarists that come to mind when thinking of the Hungarian Gypsy Minor scale. The scale is often used in Gypsy music. Those who play Middle Eastern Oud tend to use the Hungarian Gypsy Minor guitar scale.

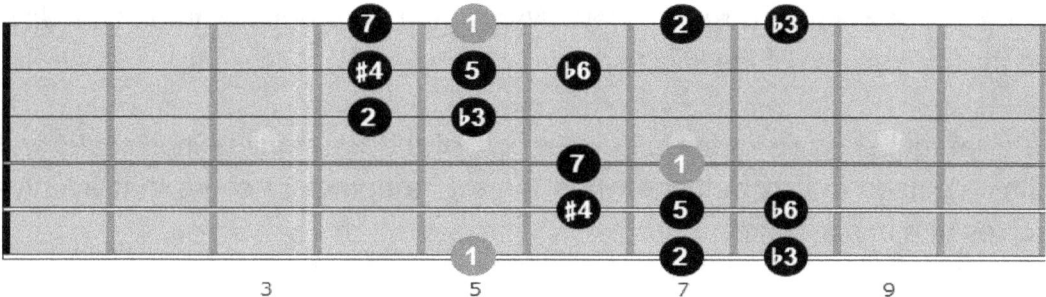

Romanian Guitar Scale

The best way to think of the Romanian Guitar scale is as a minor scale with a **#4**. The Romanian Guitar scale is often referred to as the Ukranian Dorian mode, the altered Dorian scale, or the Miserbach scale. This scale is the fourth mode in the harmonic minor scale.

It is very similar to the Dorian mode, though it uses a tritone and variable sixth/seventh degrees. The scale is often used in Klezmer music. The melodies that come from the Romanian scale are often thought of as exotic or romantic.

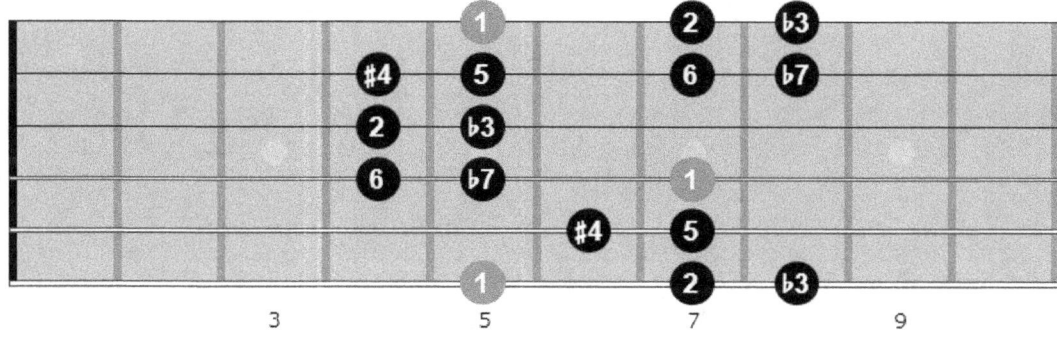

Hijaz Guitar Scale

The Hijaz Scale comes from Saudi Arabia and is a dominant scale in nature. Some refer to the Hijaz as the Jewish scale, the Spanish gypsy scale, or the Phrygian dominant scale, though the Phrygian dominant name is more of a jazz thing.

The scale can often be found in traditional Spanish songs as well, both inside and outside of the Flamenco realm. *Hava Nagila* is a very popular traditional Jewish tune that makes use of the Hijaz scale.

The Hijaz guitar scale is the fifth inversion of the harmonic minor scale and is commonly used in jazz settings when there is a dominant chord that eventually resolves to a minor chord.

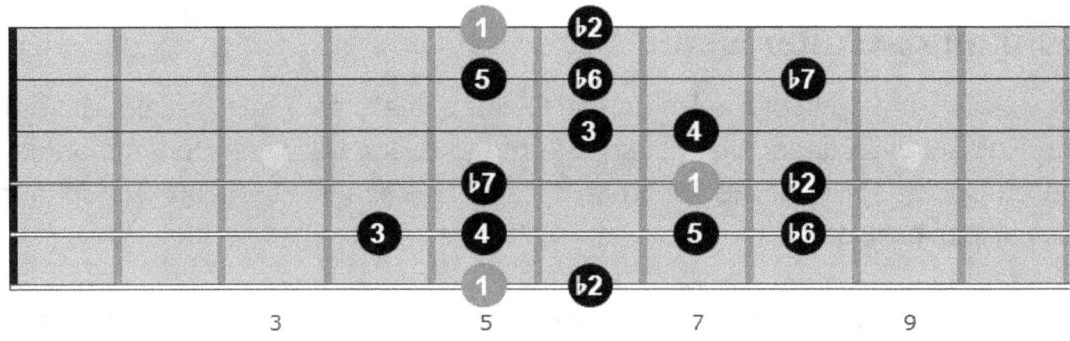

Chapter 11 - Additional Scales

Now that we have explored the popular scales and modes within the realm of guitar, let's explore a few unique scales that stand on their own.

Whole-Tone Scale

The whole-tone scale is defined as a symmetrical scale that is built using a series of whole steps in succession; it is built entirely of whole steps. The whole-tone scale is a "hexatonic scale", meaning it consists of six notes. You can divide the octave in the whole-tone scale into six equal notes. The whole-tone scale is unique because there are no half steps, so there are no leading tones available for resolution.

The whole-tone scale is often used for theatrical purposes; in film music it is often used in scenes that need the music to add suspense and mystery. Often it is used during a comedic dream sequence in shows. It is also used in jazz settings, as it helps to add a bit of tension, especially when improvising over dominant chords. The whole-tone scale does contain a raised fifth (**#5**) and a raised eleventh (**#11**) too, which provides a unique color for improvisation.

Building the Whole-Tone Scale

Let's take a look at how we build the whole tone scale. We will use the root **G** to build our scale. The interval structure is as follows:

G Whole Tone Scale - G A B C# D# F
Interval Formula - 1 2 3 #4 #5 b7
With Upper-structures - 1 9 3 #11 #5 b7

Of course, applying this scale to the fingerboard is what truly matters. If you look at the diagram below, you can see the G Whole-Tone scale:

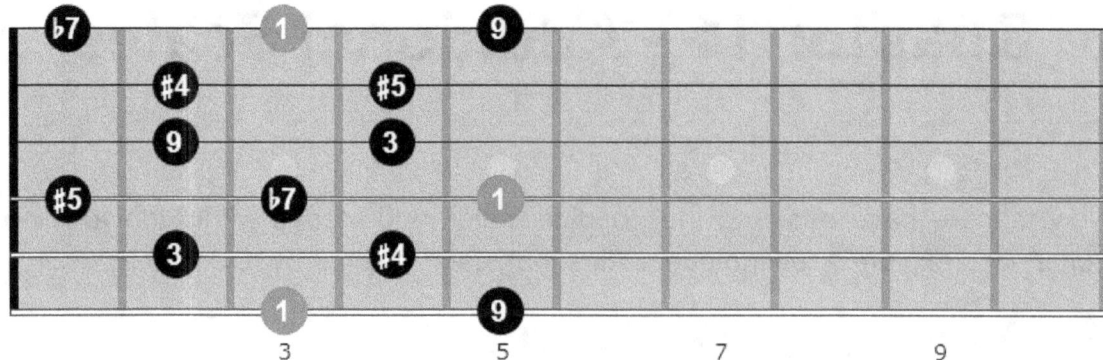

You can move this position starting from the sixth string to anywhere on the fretboard starting from the same string to play the whole-tone scale with different roots.

The next diagram is the C Whole-Tone scale, which starts on the fifth string in this case.

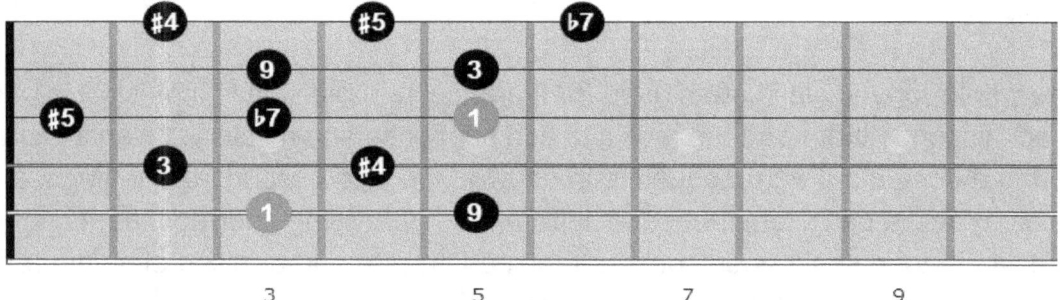

You can move this scale up and down the fretboard as well.

Practicing the Whole Tone Scale

Now that you have a better idea of the whole-tone scale, let's dig into a couple patterns that you can run through to lock the scale in. These patterns can help you expand your technique and knowledge of the whole-tone scale from the bottom to the top of the fretboard.

All of the following patterns are written in ascending order moving *up* the shape of the scale. Of course, you can *also* practice them in a descending manner if you want as well.

Whole Tone Practice Scale #1

This first whole-tone scale pattern moves up in thirds throughout the scale. You will play the first note of the scale, then the third note, then the second note, then the fourth note, and so on.

Whole Tone Practice Scale #2

The second whole-tone scale is essentially the first whole-tone scale, though in reverse. As you will see, this pattern uses a series of descending third intervals.

Whole Tone Practice Scale #3

The third whole-tone scale pattern combines the first two practice patterns. You play an ascending third to start with and a descending third next. You alternate between these two as you continue through the scale.

Whole Tone Practice Scale #4

The last whole-tone practice pattern is the third practice scale in reverse. You start with an ascending third first and move to a descending third next, alternating between the two.

The Whole Tone Scale in Popular Music

One of the very first and most popular instances of the whole tone scale in music was thanks to Johann Rudolf Ahle. He composed a piece in 1662 using the whole tone scale and was eventually followed by a number of other classical composers, including Mozart, Bach, Berlioz, Schubert, and more.

Claude Debussy, an impressionist composer, was very fond of the whole-tone scale as well. You often hear the whole-tone scale in many of his compositions, such a "Voiles". One of the most famous uses of the whole-tone scale in modern music is "You Are The Sunshine Of My Life" by Stevie Wonder. You can hear it used in the intro of the track.

Diminished Scale

Now let's move on to the **diminished scale**. The diminished scale is an octatonic (eight-note) scale that alternates in whole and half steps moving up from the root. People often refer to the diminished scale as either the whole-half or half-whole diminished scale.

There are two different patterns for the diminished scale: whole-half, which alternates whole and half steps; or half-whole, which is just the opposite. Let's take a look at how we build the whole-half diminished scale. The interval structure is as follows:

Diminished Scale - C D Eb F Gb Ab B C

Interval Formula - 1 2 b3 4 b5 b6 7 8
With Upper Structures - 1 9 b3 11 b5 #5 13 7 8

It is important to note that this diminished scale is separate from the dominant diminished scale, or the half-whole diminished scale. The dominant diminished scale alternates beginning with a half step and then a whole step, and is often used by guitarists when improvising atop 7b9 chords.

Building the Diminished Scale

To figure out your diminished scale fingerings, let's check out a shape that spans over two octaves starting from the low sixth string. We will build the scale starting from the root note **G**, meaning this is the G Diminished Scale.

Once you learn how to play the G Diminished scale starting from the sixth string, you can shift the entire scale up or down frets to play the diminished scale starting on different roots.

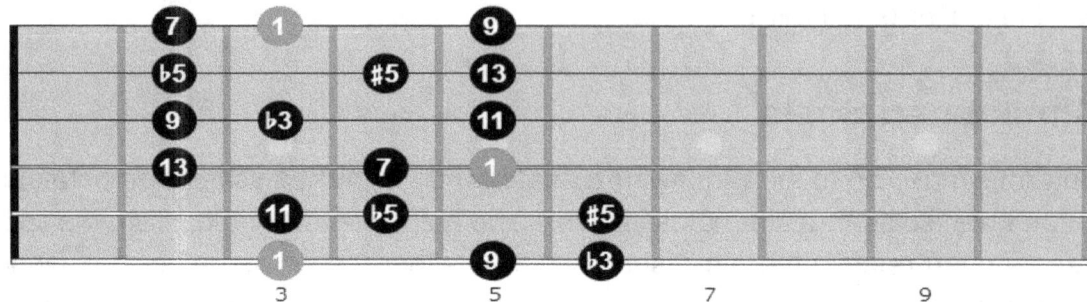

Now let's take a look at how we can play the G diminished scale starting on the fifth string on the guitar.

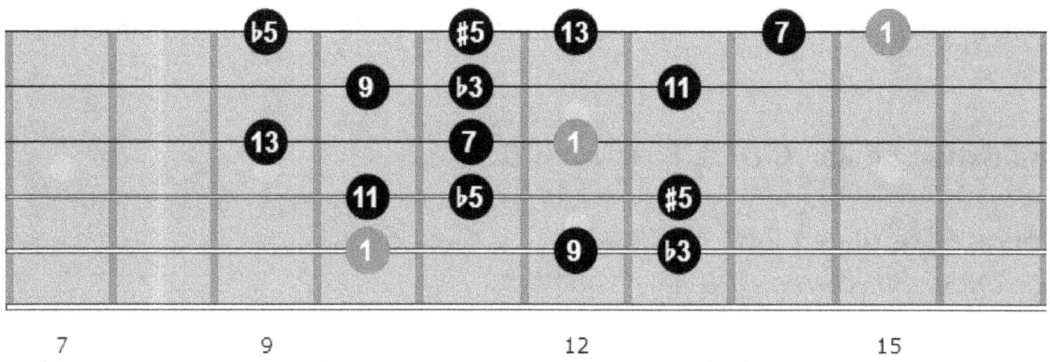

Practicing the Diminished Scale

Now that you have a good idea of how the Diminished Scale looks, let's dig in and check out a few practice variations of the diminished scale. This particular jazz pattern is known as diatonic thirds.

We can apply diatonic thirds to the G diminished scale starting from the low sixth string.

Diminished Practice Scale #1

To start out, we will check out the G Diminished scale moving in ascending thirds.

Diminished Practice Scale #2

The next practice pattern is similar to the first practice scale, though played using descending thirds instead.

Diminished Practice Scale #3

The third practice pattern for the diminished scale uses an ascending third followed by a descending third. You can think of this as an alternating third scale.

Diminished Practice Scale #4

The last practice pattern is the reverse of the third diminished practice scale. You start with the first third descending, followed by the next third ascending, and so on.

Chapter 12 - Practicing Your Scales

Congratulations!

You've made it through all of the scales in the book!

Scales are the vocabulary of music, and it is incredibly important to practice them. With scales, we can produce different emotions and sounds. If you learn to use scales effectively, you can create a mood and vibe for songwriters and singers to work with, you can write your own music with confidence and intention, and you will share an understanding with other musicians of this important concept.

The unfortunate thing is that many guitarists practice scales without knowing exactly **why** they are practicing or what they are looking to accomplish by doing so; this can be endlessly frustrating for guitar players. Some guitarists may find themselves unsure of how to use the material they practiced in a practical musical environment.

We always recommend creating clear goals for yourself when you are practicing, especially when practicing your scales. Remember, we don't have an infinite amount of time to practice the guitar; that is why it is so important not to waste any of that precious time!

So the question is, why is it important to practice scales?

For starters, practicing will enable you to internalize the *sound* of a scale. When you begin creating your own melodies, you'll have a better concept of practical application, since melodies are built using notes within scales. As you build a strong inner-ear, thanks to internalizing the sound of a scale, it can help you to transcribe solos byear, since knowing your scales can help you narrow down your transcription to seven notes (unless we're talking about some of those pentatonic or octatonic scales!).

For those who play lead guitar or like to improvise guitar riffs, all of the exercises that we will discuss are made to help with improvisation and creativity. Improvisation is a necessary skill for those who want to play professionally in live settings. Great improvisation can lead to greater jam sessions!

Lastly, implementing a scale practice routine into your general practice will help build up your accuracy and dexterity, similar to many guitar exercises.

Just remember, there are many different scales that exist in the musical world. We have found that it is much better to have one scale on lock rather than *sort of* understanding six or seven scales. Make sure you take your time when learning each scale; you can get a lot of mileage out of them if you split up your tasks for every scale (patterns one day, note names next, creating pattern routines, etc.).

Now, let's give you some material to practice!

Ascending and Descending Exercises

The ascending and descending exercise pattern is one of the most common ways of practicing scales. You simply start on the lowest note of your chosen scale and move throughout the scale's notes until you reach the highest possible note, then move backwards down the scale to the root that you started on.

We recommend doing these ascending and descending scales in two octaves. The ascending and descending exercises help you to build your muscle memory so that you can remember where the notes of each scale lie. Make sure to practice with a metronome or quantized drum loop, listening for accuracy; and of course, start slow and move up in speed as you become more comfortable.

Changing Directions

The next exercise is very similar to the ascending and descending exercises, though instead of ascending or descending to the highest and lowest notes in the scale, you pick places where you want to change direction; make sure that you don't skip any notes in the scale when you change directions.

Let's say that you are moving in ascending order and your plan is to change directions once you reach the fifth degree of the scale. On the way back down, you will start your descent on the fourth degree of the scale. Lots of people who practice in this way tend to accidentally skip notes when they begin their direction change, especially if the next note sits on an adjacent string.

Practice on One String

Let's face it, the guitar is not the most visual instrument around. It can be quite difficult to make sense of how the guitar is laid out note-wise, especially if we practice most of our scales in box patterns. Think of a piano for a moment, as it is a much better visual representation of our musical notes.

You can easily *see* the C Major scale on the piano; since the C major scale is all natural notes, with no sharps or flats, it is laid out on the white keys moving from C to C. There it is, simple! It is a very visual instrument.
The guitar, on the other hand, is often thought of as a bunch of patterns that change as you move up the neck.

That is why it seems like there are so many scales to learn. Of course, memorizing all of these scales is a feat. For some, it's nearly impossible. Luckily, there are a few ways to combat the idea of pattern memorization.

To do so, I highly recommend practicing a few of your scales using only one string, up and down the neck.

When you play a scale on one string, you connect the formula of the scale to the visual aspect of guitar playing. It's a unique way to approach scales, though it is highly effective. Let's look at the major scale formula, for example:

W-W-H-W-W-W-H

The above pattern says that the major scale has a whole-step moving from the root to the second. That second is followed by a half-step, then a whole-step, and so on.

If we look at the E Major scale, we get this:

E-F#-G#-A-B-C#-D#-E

If we were to play the E Major scale on one string, adding an extra open-E to breathe some fresh air into the basic scale pattern, we would get this:

Then, you can play it in reverse, add some extra open E string hits to create some Celtic flair, or work on your strumming/picking technique. Do note that this is definitely **not** the only way you should be practicing your scales, though it is very helpful for visualizing how a scale fits on the neck of the guitar.

Note Sequences

The note sequences scale exercise is great for building a better mental image of the scale. You want to start your note sequence practice by choosing the number of notes that you will play in your sequence.

For example, let's say that you decide to make your sequence with five notes. You will start your sequence on the root note of the scale and play up until you have reached the fifth scale degree.
The next portion of the sequence will start on the second scale degree and end on the sixth scale degree. Next, you will start on the third scale degree and end on

the seventh scale degree. Essentially, you are playing using groups or sequences of five notes. You will continue to move through this pattern until you get to the highest note in the scale.

Rhythmically, you can put a little rest between each portion of this exercise, or find ways to make it your own by not using any space.

If you are a bit confused, you can think of the sequences like this:

- **1 2 3 4 5**
- **2 3 4 5 6**
- **3 4 5 6 7**
- **4 5 6 7 1**
- **5 6 7 1 2**
- **6 7 1 2 3**
- **7 1 2 3 4**

The numbers above represent the degrees of the scale, and in this exercise we are using sequences of five. You can change the number of notes in the sequence very easily. Often this exercise climbs in groups of three, four, or five.

Intervals

To start the interval exercise, you must first choose an interval to work with; For this example, we will use thirds. You will start on the lowest root note and move up a third from that note. You will then hop back down to the second scale degree of that particular scale and then move up a third from there. You will continue to hop back down to the third scale degree, then a third up from that, then back down to the fourth scale degree, then up a third from there.

Here is the interval pattern:
1-3-2-4-3-5-4-6-5-7-6-8-7-9-8

Drone Practice

One of the best ways to practice exotic guitar scales, or any unique scales for that matter, is with a drone. Sometimes called a pedal tone, a drone is a note or chord that is continuously sounded, similar to a bag-pipes "bag". If you want to practice your exotic guitar scales, I highly recommend practicing with a drone. While it is very important for a guitarist to understand the relationships between scales and chords, it is just as important to visualize scales with a more horizontal understanding.

When you play with a drone, you have a bit more room for figuring out how notes and harmonies work with one another. Instead of concentrating on when to change notes when certain chords come about, playing with a drone allows you to focus on finding the best-sounding chord tones.

You can experiment with different style elements, nuances, or colors, that sit within different keys. This method is used often in traditional Indian music. An instrument called the tanpura will play a continuous harmonic drone to support the melody of another instrument, which is typically the sitar.

You can find drone tracks on a wide variety of media, including stand-alone audio tracks or cello drones on YouTube. Of course, you can also make your own. The key is that a drone track should be simple and long. The idea is that you have all of the time you need to completely internalize a scale and make adjustments to your tones as you move along.

Simply play through your scales atop a drone, moving step-wise, then skipping strings, then devising your own melodies. This is a fun way to step out of the box. In a way, it almost doesn't feel like practice at all; it is a meditation in nature and can be a very soothing, healthy practice tool.

The next set of scale practice exercises work to help you integrate your knowledge of scales into a context that is musical. So many beginner guitarists have a bad habit of improvising by simply running up and down scales. If your solos sound like scale exercises, there won't be any life or musical expression for a listener to feel in your playing. These exercises can help bring a bit more spice into your sound.

Utilize Nursery Rhymes

Nursery rhymes are great for practicing any instrument, as they make use of simple melodies that are easy to grasp. Using your major scale, pick a nursery rhyme and play it. You can start from various places in your major scales too, playing your chosen nursery rhyme from the root, second, third, fourth, fifth, and so on.

Here are a few nursery rhymes that you can try out:

- **Hot Cross Bun**
- **Mary Had A Little Lamb**
- **Baa, Baa, Black Sheep**
- **Twinkle, Twinkle, Little Star**
- **Itsy Bitsy Spider**
- **Row, Row, Row Your Boat**

Other fun melodies to incorporate in this type of practice:

- **We Will Rock You**
- **Eye of the Tiger**
- **Smoke on the Water**
- **Mission Impossible**
- **Seven Nation Army**
- **My House (bassline)**

Sing While You Play

A very important part of being a good musician is the ability to match pitch; it doesn't matter if you feel that you have a bad singing voice, no excuses! Start by playing a simple phrase on the guitar, then play it again while matching the same notes with your voice. Then, progress to playing a whole phrase and singing it back, or improvising back and forth with the guitar and your voice; have some fun!

The idea behind the singing and playing exercise is that it shortens the time between your thoughts and your actions. Practicing these types of ideas has the potential to unlock a lot of musical creativity, and bring more emotion and "soul" into your solos.

Transcription

One of the most important exercises for any musician is the ability to transcribe. Transcribing, for those of you who don't know, is the act of listening to a piece of music and writing out the notes as you hear them. You can either use musical notation or tablature to do this.

Initially, you may find the act of transcribing pretty difficult, though as you continue doing it, you'll be able to pick out notes and intervals as if it were second nature. Start by listening to some of your favorite guitarists or guitar solos and try to transcribe exactly what you are hearing with your ears. We find that it helps to sing the notes out loud when you are transcribing as well!

Eventually, you will become good enough at transcribing that you will be able to do it in your head.

Improvisation

Improvisation is the final exercise to practice. Many people improvise with backing tracks, as it helps to provide the feeling of playing within a real band setting. Of course, you don't *need* to play with a backing track if you don't want to.

Improvising can simply mean noodling along within a certain scale. It can sometimes be more beneficial to do this first, then move on to play with a backing track once you are more comfortable with the scale.

Try backing tracks that use different scales and modes. Try to play around in different genres to get a feel for different types of improvisation. Improvisation is one of the most rewarding forms of practice, hands down. It WILL make you a better guitarist.

Conclusion

Thank you so much for reading along./! We sincerely hope that you are able to practice these scales and become a better guitarist.

Music is a truly endless journey. There are hundreds of different scales and exercises out there, though we believe this book provides the perfect starting point for guitarists who want enough information to become versatile players without feeling overwhelmed.

As a takeaway, we recommend going back and practicing these scales one at a time. Try to master one scale before moving on to the next. Playing guitar is a bit like riding a bike: once you have internalized a scale or series of notes, your brain will be able to recall them at the drop of a hat.

Don't rush yourself and you'll be surprised how much your technique improves!

Good luck and happy shredding!

www.ingramcontent.com/pod-product-compliance
Lightning Source LLC
Chambersburg PA
CBHW081750100526
44592CB00015B/2373